Cooperation at Work

The Mondragon Experience

Keith Bradley
*London School of Economics and Wharton School,
University of Pennsylvania*

Alan Gelb
World Bank

Heinemann Educational Books

Heinemann Educational Books Ltd
22 Bedford Square, London WC1B 3HH
LONDON EDINBURGH MELBOURNE AUCKLAND
HONG KONG SINGAPORE KUALA LUMPUR NEW DELHI
IBADAN NAIROBI JOHANNESBURG
EXETER (NH) KINGSTON PORT OF SPAIN

British Library Cataloguing in Publication Data

Bradley, Keith
    Co-operation at work: the Mondragon experience.
    1. Cooperation—Spain—Mondragon
    2. Mondragon (Spain)—Industries
    I. Title   II. Gelb, Alan
    334'.6'094661   HD2888.5.M6/

ISBN 0-435-83109-7
ISBN 0-435-83110-0 Pbk

Phototypesetting by The Castlefield Press, Moulton, Northampton
Printed in Great Britain by Biddles Ltd, Guildford, Surrey

Cooperation at Work

By the same authors
Worker Capitalism: the New Industrial Relations

Contents

Preface

In the present search for new forms of industrial organisation and workplace consensus, worker cooperatives assert themselves as experiments worthy of study. None more than Mondragon, the largest, most complete and perhaps most successful cooperative in a capitalist economy. This book grew out of a desire that Mondragon's experience contribute to the debate on the directions which industrial relations should follow.

We particularly wish to thank Nuria Batlle, Michael Mann and Robert Oakeshott for assistance and suggestions for research, also Chris Clamp and Jan Svejnar. Caroline's discipline contributed significantly to the well-being and presence of mind of the authors. Empirical research at Mondragon has been helped and rendered pleasant by the openness and cooperation of the people who live and work in the area, on cooperatives and firms. For their time and assistance we especially thank Iñaki Aguirre, Anton Calleja, Iñaki Gorroño and Rafael Fernandez.

It is difficult to do justice in a brief note to the skills of Aludia Oropesa, who, quite unfazed by intense pressure, produced the manuscript with startling efficiency.

The book is dedicated to Gloria who inspired both the authors.

Finally, we acknowledge the support of the Nuffield Foundation.

April 1983

1 The Cost of Conflict

The New Challenge
In the United States, Britain and other major Western industrial countries traditional sectors and methods of industrial organization face their most serious challenge since the Great Depression of the 1930s. The Corporate Economy is under stress, paradoxically in a political environment more conservative, on the whole, than that of the booming sixties or turbulent seventies. Industrial decline was until recently limited to a few specific industries (notably textiles) and to restricted geographic areas. It has now spread to encompass former leading sectors – automobiles, shipbuilding, machine tools, appliances and a wide range of associated products – and to include regions recently prosperous. Not all of this trend can be reversed, or should be. Partly, it reflects a general tendency for demand patterns to shift towards services with rising incomes and inevitable changes in comparative advantage. In the long run, it may no longer be efficient to mass-produce a wide range of manufactures in the richest countries. But, as suggested by numerous debates on the need to 'reindustrialize', at least part of the decline of Western manufacturing is felt to result from an undue decrease in competitiveness of industry relative to that of Japan and the newly industrialized countries.[1] Poor performance of Western industry manifested in productivity slowdown increases the stress of adjustment by accelerating relative productivity change and simultaneously reducing growth making adjustment more difficult.

Corporate management has always sought to raise efficiency. But perceptions that established industries are falling behind are intensifying efforts to improve the organization of production. The search horizon of management is broadening dramatically, as traditional philosophies are brought into question. Barely a decade ago, it was a rare American or British manager who felt it necessary to appraise critically his established principles. Now, management innovates, eagerly studies the experiments of rival firms and travels abroad for inspiration. The corporate economy is not about to transform itself by adopting new, untested techniques. But the 1980s promise a watershed in industrial structure and organization. The direction of change is clear. Expansionist Keynesian demand-management is no longer able to underwrite the cost of conflict, in terms of lost production and unemployment, generated by traditional collective bargaining. With limited resources and tight monetary policy, traditional arrangements are increasingly seen as a zero sum (or negative sum) game, where one man's wage hike is another's unemployment and industrial strife encourages migration of capital. The 'new industrial relations' emphasizes labor-capital consensus which must be fostered by the appropriate incentive structures within the firm. The focus is shifted away from collective bargaining while trade unions face a more constrained and difficult set of choices. With high unemployment it is more likely that the quest for consensus will extend outside the firm to include increasingly dependent communities.

This book deals with one significant industrial experiment featuring radically different patterns of ownership and control and situated in a capitalist environment – the Mondragon group of worker cooperatives in the Basque provinces of Spain. Since its inception in 1956, Mondragon's record has been enviable. It has grown rapidly. From virtually every perspective, it appears to have outperformed the local capitalist environment. Of particular interest to the ageing traditional zones most affected by 'deindustrialization', it has acted as a focus for regional development. What lessons can be drawn from Mondragon for traditionally structured capitalist industry, for regional development, and indeed for industrialization strategy in general? This success record may not argue for the adoption of cooperative structures in their totality. However, Mondragon's organization, performance and potential makes it a useful laboratory for assessing alternative firm structures sharing many features of the new industrial relations.

In a small way Mondragon is already influencing policy, despite having only been 'discovered' by a wide audience in 1977. Economic stagnation in the 1970s has encouraged a trend towards employee buyouts of declining firms. This has been most marked in the US, but recently has reacquired momentum in Britain after a lull following the disastrous experiences of the 1974 cooperatives encouraged by the Labour government.[2] Mondragon did not cause this trend, nor shape the rules of ownership and control in the new enterprises. But its existence has added legitimacy to their struggle for acceptance, and it has influenced American and British legislation dealing with cooperative enterprises. Responding to extreme unemployment and a perceived need to 'reindustrialize' the depressed region of South Wales, in 1980 the British government initiated a study to assess the applicability of the Mondragon model to such declining areas. The industrial policy of the new Social Democratic Party in Britain has been influenced by Mondragon. So has been cooperative legislation in Massachusetts and indirectly, other American cooperative legislation.[3]

Mondragon is of interest for pragmatic, rather than purely ideological considerations. Contrary to the predictions of the 1960s that slower growth would generate a radical backlash among the working (or unemployed) classes, the slowdown of the 1980s has resulted in a surprisingly limited ideological challenge to traditional Western-style capitalism. Rather, debate has been expressed in terms of jobs and real incomes. Reducing unemployment, avoiding real wage cuts and bringing down inflation – albeit by a few points – have preoccupied governments and trade unions alike. In this environment, attacks on *formal* private ownership of the means of production have been of no consequence. More significant has been the tendency to question existing property rights prevailing within industrial enterprises, and the functions and prerogatives of management. At first sight, the ideological vacuum is advantageous to capitalism. But because criticism is pragmatic (how can management claim the right to manage if it is unable to maintain viability in the marketplace?) and because the managerial class too is suffering the cost of economic decline, the problems are particularly challenging. Labor is not staging an ideological mutiny against management. Increasingly, it seeks leadership in raising industrial productivity. Implementing this partnership is a task at the heart of the new labor relations.

Industrial Alternatives: the Resurgence of Pluralism

It has been clear, since Marx, that Western industry was developing asymmetrically, in identifying 'the firm' exclusively with the owners of its capital stock, rather than with some combination of productive factors. Capital has been 'personalized' as a factor of production and accorded the sole right of organization. Labor, on the other hand, has been depersonalized to a similar factoral status but is denied a similar measure of responsibility. Thus, capital hires and fires labor rather than labor capital or some more symmetrical contract. At the turn of the 20th century this trend towards capital control was formalized by the 'scientific management' school of industrial organization into a technically advanced system for reducing labor to a subordinate role. Through progressive job fragmentation scientific management eroded subcontracting practices widespread in early capitalist development, and evolved its own ideology based on the separation of industrial planning and doing.

Marx probably underestimated the capacity of capitalism to adapt. Adversarial behavior is recognized as contributing to lower productivity, and for many years attempts have been made to reverse or modify these attitudes within the framework of management strategies. Until recently, traditional collective bargaining remained, however, the fulcrum of the system, with management viewing improved attitudes as an indication of better control rather than sharing of responsibility.

Distributing responsibility and worker involvement to include a greater number of employees than the small managerial elite has far-reaching consequences for labor relations. In the process the firm becomes more like a community. This requires an employment contract enriched beyond the wage transaction; the defining characteristic of any community is a system, usually fairly complex, of reciprocal rights and obligations. Production cannot then be separated from social relationships within the firm. Once this is accepted, a firm may also be more receptive towards external community ties in general. It may, of course, be extremely difficult to change attitudes within a firm and there is no guarantee that attempts to share responsibility will harmonise industrial relations and improve productivity. Particularly when introduced at times of extreme economic stress they may be viewed by labour as simply another management device.[4]

What has impelled the new trend to alternative organization? There appear to be three main factors. Social developments in the industrial countries have combined with technical change to render conventional methods of organization and control less effective. The impact has been accelerated by the example of Japan.

Social factors include an increased reluctance to accept the fundamental tradeoff of scientific management – total surrender of individual discretion for monetary reward – with greater prosperity and social security. It is increasingly difficult to reconcile autocratic management practices *within* firms with democratic political structures *outside* in a period where the latter have emphasized increasing participation. Political concern for the rights of individuals and social groups raises expectations. It spills over into the industrial arena, making the environment more difficult for traditional management. In the United States such concerns have led to pressure on companies to demonstrate equitable personnel policies, sometimes in the face of conflicting regulations. Trends in Europe have been more concerned with protecting the rights of workers as a class (rather than as individual members of groups), and management faces tighter limits than in the United States. Growing restriction has not always involved legislation. Britain, for example, lacks the American legal framework for collective bargaining. A voluntary system of industrial relations combined with job legislation until recently, to limit managerial control. In practice, a wide set of decisions was considered to organized labor. Both Labour and Conservative governments have attempted to move towards the American legislative model against union opposition.

The second factor undermining traditional organization has been technological change. This has led to the shrinkage of the blue-collar work force and to the encroachment of new methods of control on lower echelons of white-collar workers and management. For a considerable period, the more dynamic industrial sectors in the richer countries have been those dependent on human capital. Excluding farm and personal service workers, in 1920 there were 1.6 blue-collar workers for each white-collar worker in the US. By 1980 this proportion had declined to 0.6, at which stage the traditional classification was dropped from the US statistics. Although white-collar workers have not escaped scientific management (especially at lower levels), such occupations are harder to monitor through established methods, as demonstrated by the relative slowness with which scientific management has permeated the service sectors. The increasing role of human capital has blurred the traditionally sharp divide between manual blue-collar production workers and technocratic management operating with a wide range of discretion. Looking ahead to the introduction of robotics into industry, many of the occupations routine enough to be easily monitored are also routine enough not to require workers at all.

Both technical and social factors therefore argue for a trend away from enforcement of corporate goals on reluctant workers towards voluntary alignment of individual goals with corporate objectives. Improved incentive structures, rather than more elaborate job controls, are the hallmark of the new industrial relations.

Successful Japanese penetration of Western markets over the 1970s despite relatively slow market growth is the third factor. It focused attention abruptly on the limitations of traditional scientific management techniques in Western industry. Increases in Japanese industrial productivity during the 1950s and early 1960s were easy to attribute to the modernization and reconstruction of the economy following the Second World War. By 1972, Japanese levels of industrial technology were estimated to have caught up to those of the United States.[5] Japanese industry nevertheless continued to outperform Western industry. Japan ran trade surpluses of $85 billion over the 1970s and expanded aggressively into new product lines and markets despite the increasing costs of imported energy.

A large measure of this success has been attributed to the organization of major Japanese corporations, which combine paternalism and bureaucracy in a distinctive synthesis. Large Japanese corporations expect to employ members for life, base wages on age as well as merit and are committed to looking after the 'whole man'. The extent to which this 'paternalistic-lifetime commitment' production relationship reflects deliberate choice or evolved from Japan's social tradition and recent industrialization is still debated. Whatever its cause, superior Japanese industrial performance is widely held to reflect its characteristic labor relations system which has been recognized as aligning individual goals closely with that of the corporation. The demonstration effect on Western management has been striking.

The case for alternative organization need not turn on Japan alone. Certain major Western companies – termed Z firms by Ouchi (1982) – have cultivated a labor environment resembling that of the Japanese corporations. They have experienced success in the marketplace as well as maintained generally superior employee relations; while this may not prove causality it certainly shows that the two objectives are not incompatible. Not unlike the Japanese corporations, they marry human and technical dimensions of the production process through distinctive company philosophies which embody a degree of enterprise paternalism. These firms derive their management style from a tradition independent of that of Japan. In fact, Western paternalistic industrial relationships extend back to the Industrial Revolution. They were instrumental in shaping the first stages of transformation to industrial societies. Particularly significant were the social experiments of Robert Owen, which proceeded on both sides of the Atlantic at New Lanark and New Hampshire. Owen sought to raise industrial efficiency by social prescriptions which adapted the surrounding environment of the firm to the needs of the production process. He was succeeded by the Rochdale Pioneers who established the first successful British cooperative, and influenced a Quaker tradition of paternalist industrial organization which is still manifested in a number of leading British companies.[6]

Owen's views and writings combined with Catholic social doctrine to exert a powerful influence on the founder of Mondragon, Don Jose Maria Arizmendi. Mondragon seeks to integrate the community and the production process, and displays some important characteristics of Japanese corporations and Western 'Z firms'. In many respects it differs from these examples. Because Mondragon is a group of cooperatives it secures its sense of a productive community through distinctive economic and social mechanisms. It therefore points to another structure to be examined for its potential to implement consensus and promote efficient patterns of industrial relations.

Mondragon does more, however. It has been suggested that the

Japanese corporations have been able to operate in an environment which, relative to that of the West, is unusually tolerant of social hierarchy. Japan has seen little resistance to the rights of capital, because labor markets are segmented between the privileged third who work for major industrial corporations and the weakly organized remainder. Within the corporations, the need to maintain consensus limits the way in which capital is able to exercise its rights. Slow development of the Japanese social security system is probably symbolic of labor's failure to assert itself as a independent force. In contrast, the postwar history of Western industrial relations – at least in Europe – can be seen as increasing encroachment of organized labor on capital's prerogatives through the political process, a challenge which has not gone unresisted by capital. In the United States unions are traditionally more pragmatic, and powerful only in a limited set of activities, yet they too have fought to limit management rights. The result has been capital flight to the less unionized South and West and weakened industry in traditional centers.[7] Mondragon, like other worker-owned enterprises, has sought to abolish the capital-labor distinction, establishing *ab initio* the conditions for integrated communal production processes. Against the historic trend of Western industrial development it represents a second useful norm of alternative organization.

The Importance of the Cooperative Example
To date, producer cooperatives have played only a peripheral role in major industrialized economies. They have invariably been small, often outside major industrial centers and although there are exceptions, have rarely survived for substantial periods. As far back as the Webbs (1921), cooperatives have been viewed with skepticism as unable to survive in a sea of capitalism. They face obstacles to capital accumulation, and the few dynamic examples have tended to degenerate into traditional capitalist firms. They appear to be doomed to short, inconsequential lives. In no industrial country (except Yugoslavia if considered in the group) have production cooperatives played a major role. A number of the developing countries motivated by a desire to find an alternative to socialism and capitalism have experimented with cooperatisation. The results have often been disastrous. The successful Mondragon experiment nevertheless is worthy of study for three reasons.

Firstly, in Western firms an important component of many attempts to improve industrial relations has been the extension of equity ownership to rank and file employees. This contrasts with the Japanese practice of providing incentives through annual profit-related bonuses.

In the United States at least, this trend has been bolstered by two independent movements encouraging employee ownership of equity. By 1980 thirteen separate pieces of legislation had been passed facilitating the transfer of equity to workforces through Employee Stock Ownership Plans (ESOPs).[8] Some 4000 firms have taken advantage of this option. The ESOP is a long way from worker control. Shares are held beneficially through a trust rather than directly by individual employees and there is no automatic link between ownership and worker participation. Further, a major incentive for companies to adopt an ESOP is favorable tax treatment of deductions signed over to the Employee Stock Ownership Trust through which stock is distributed. Nevertheless ESOP legislation stems from a desire to render the distribution of wealth more equitable. It also reflects the reaction against monopoly capitalism characteristic of the populist small-business ethic. This has been a powerful factor in American ideology.[9]

Employees buyouts of their declining firms, mostly dating from the start of the 1970s, constitute another trend towards worker ownership. Often hastily planned and conceived with little regard for the implications of new ownership structures for control, these attempts to save jobs have extended direct employee share ownership over a wide spectrum of industries. This trend should not be underestimated – such takeovers are judged to have saved directly between 50,000 and 100,000 jobs over the 1970s in the US alone. This estimate excludes many sizeable buyouts in the 1980s and less complete, yet quantitatively greater transitions to partial employee stock ownership in certain large companies. Notable cases here include the Chrysler rescue and the reconstruction of Pan American Airlines.

Secondly, in addition to their role in redistributing capital away from monopoly ownership, cooperatives are a source of increased labor flexibility. They fragment and weaken national or industry-wide collective bargaining. This is not to say that worker ownership necessarily means the end of unions. Employee ownership in the United States has typically coexisted with unionism, although this is probably due to the fact that ownership has almost never changed the pattern of control towards true industrial democracy. However, the role of the union shifts with employee ownership. From opposition, it has necessarily to become more constructive in its dealings with the firm. The potential shift in priorities of local union branches following employee ownership is anticipated by the tension between national and local union organizations upon the prospect of employee buyouts. Local union leadership, sometimes faced with the alternative of painful redundancy and loss of membership, has pragmatically accepted and sometimes supported employee ownership. National union leadership has been more concerned with maintaining traditional collective bargaining which is both the mainspring of trade unionism and a major obstacle to rationalization and the introduction of new technology.

The British case suggests that realignment of local union goals may be more important to harmonize industrial relations than reducing the power of national over firm-level unionism. British industrial relations became more difficult and anarchic with the rise of the shop stewards movement in the 1960s and weakening of national union power. Local union attitudes did not shift towards those of enterprise unionism following the recommendation of Donovan (1968) that power be institutionalized at local level. The prime goal is not the location of power but is to realign union objectives at plant level. To what extent can a move towards worker ownership accomplish this?

Finally, Mondragon's own record of growth, employment creation, capital accumulation and investment in human skills renders it an outstanding regional development institution, as outlined in more detail below. Cooperatives are not necessarily statically inefficient in the sense that their current operating costs exceed those of conventional firms. In fact there is some evidence that the reverse can be true. But however efficient, they appear to be organizationally unstable over time. Mondragon's record so far suggests an ability to counter long-run degenerative tendencies common to cooperatives. Does it provide a way to combine the best features of static efficiency and dynamic growth – and if so, in what socio-political environments?

This book attempts to assess the Mondragon experiment as one model of industrial organization. What lessons does it indicate for attempts to improve industrial relations and to raise productivity through restructuring the ownership of assets? Does it provide a useful model for reindustrialization of mature regions or for promoting industrialization in developing economies? How, if at all, is its commercial success related to its organization? Finally, can it be sustained over long periods and replicated in a variety of industrial societies?

Overview

The following chapter briefly describes the Mondragon experiment and reviews its structure, its record of growth and its history of employment creation. From one perspective Mondragon is an aberration: a uniquely successful worker cooperative. However, it can be compared to the Japanese corporations and Western Z-firms and its success understood from the vantage point of consensus. This is done in Chapter 3. Mondragon is compared with conventional Western firms, with those belonging to the new paternalistic school and the Japanese corporations. While Mondragon is indeed distinctive in terms of ownership structure and differs in many respects from other firms, it comes closer to 'paternalist-lifetime-commitment' enterprises in terms of industrial relations.

Our analysis of Mondragon draws on a series of surveys conducted over a period of 18 months. This involved widescale surveys of cooperative workforces complemented by in-depth interviewing of key management, as outlined in Chapter 4. Two local conventional firms outside the cooperative group were also surveyed to provide comparators. The surveys sought to assess relationships between Mondragon's organizational structure and its efficiency, and the methods by which consensus is generated and maintained. The specificity of the cooperatives to their Basque environment, their stability over time and their potential replicability were also of major concern.

A central objective of the new industrial relations is to foster high trust between management and other employees. Therefore Chapter 5 begins with the issue of trust on Mondragon between workers, cooperative management and its central source of capital, the Caja Laboral Popular. Next, how is a favourable climate of industrial relations reflected in the operations of Mondragon? This is the subject of Chapter 6, which discusses the issues of worker monitoring, incentives and mutual support. Together, these two chapters can be considered as dealing with factors affecting production efficiency at a point in time.

In Chapter 7 the interactions between Mondragon's environment, growth and its industrial organization are examined. What local features appear to be particularly conducive to cooperative success, and which are less easily duplicated? Certain features of Mondragon's surroundings seem to have facilitated unusually rapid capital accumulation, but to have done so at the cost of limiting labor mobility. Limited mobility creates the danger of organizational stagnation, with adverse long-run implications for the absorption and generation of new technology. The age profile of Mondragon's cooperateurs implies that this problem has yet to be faced. The Group's 'open door' policy of soliciting ideas for new firms and products from outside the family of existing cooperatives may provide a safety valve if product diversity and growth are maintained.

Most organizations engage in some form of personnel selection. Usually the more successful have a larger pool of potential applicants and can apply a more rigorous screening process. That of major Japanese corporations begins at kindergarten stage, with ferocious competition to enrol children into selected schools which promise entry to privileged firms. Mondragon is less elitist in its screening but also emphasizes social codes and the integration of the individual with the local community in selecting from a wide pool of applicants. Social criteria are also weighted in promotion. In Chapter 8 we investigate the mechanisms and impact of the screening of new applicants to Mondragon, and the contributions of such screening, and of the socialization processes in maintaining cooperative consensus.

Chapter 9 summarizes conclusions. A conceptual framework for analyzing motivation and control on the cooperatives is outlined in an Annex.

2 Mondragon: History and Organization

Origins and Growth

By the time the Mondragon cooperatives began to attract attention, they were already well established. Thomas and Logan (1982) cite the first Spanish reference to Ulgor in 1967. Oakeshott introduced the Mondragon experiment to the English-speaking public in 1973. Subsequent analyses are due to Campbell, *et al.* (1977), Oakeshott (1978), Eaton (1978) and Johnson and Whyte (1977). The most extensive analysis to date is that of Thomas and Logan (1982).

During the Civil War the Basques had supported the Spanish government against the rebel army of General Franco. Franco's victory left the Basque provinces in the North of Spain devastated, including the ancient capital of Guernica destroyed in a single air-raid. Thousands of Basques fled the country, others became prisoners. Among these was a student priest, Jose Maria Arizmendi, who had worked on *Eguna*, an anti-Franco trade union paper. After the war he returned to the theological college at Vitoria to finish his studies for the priesthood. He was also interested in sociology and economics, and studied Catholic social doctrine which rejected both the laissez-faire capitalism of Adam Smith and the state collectivism of Marx. The desired alternative would reconcile social justice with individual property and freedom. Arizmendi was prevented by the German occupation from continuing his studies in Belgium and was sent by his bishop to the parish of Mondragon instead.

Before the war Mondragon had been prosperous: it was now poor and in ruins, and suffering Franco's repression. Arizmendi's first job as curate was to teach young apprentices in the school run by Union Carrejera, the major local firm. Frustrated by its limited scope, in 1943 he started his own apprentice school financed by local contributions. Arizmendi was familiar with the ideas of Owen, and with the principles adopted by the Rochdale Pioneers, a trade-unionist Christian socialist group who, influenced by Owen, had founded the first successful cooperative in Britain in 1844. Older villagers found Arizmendi's ideas hard to follow, but five of his pupils, who had become engineers attempted to introduce a degree of worker participation at Union Carrejera. The management refused and backed by the inspiration of Arizmendi and financial support of the villagers the five started their own Mondragon factory, Ulgor (an amalgam of the initial letters of their names), in 1956, producing paraffin heaters and cookers. Then followed a period of four years during which time there was a search for a suitable enterprise statute within the framework of cooperative law. Other local cooperatives were simultaneously developing, and established close ties with Ulgor. They found that they faced three common problems: (a) inadequate access to capital and managerial expertise, (b) exclusion from the Spanish Social Security System, and (c) a limited technological base.

The solution to the first two problems was to found a cooperative savings bank, the *Caja Laboral Popular* in 1959. The Caja differed from the producer cooperatives in that it had the manufacturing cooperatives as well as individuals as members. It is therefore termed a second degree cooperative. By 1980 it had 300,000 deposit accounts, providing capital to be invested in the cooperative group. This expanded rapidly. By 1980 there were more than 80 industrial cooperatives employing some 18,000 members in a diverse spectrum of activities. The product range includes machine tools, refrigerators and other kitchen applicances, furniture, bicycles, electrical components and bus bodies. Some cooperatives are agricultural but the group is mainly industrial. About 10 percent of total jobs resulted from the conversion of existing firms to cooperatives; the rest involved job creation. The Caja included also an Entrepreneural Division of specialists to help establish and maintain the growth of cooperatives. It provided accounting control and a range of management functions which could be called on by the individual cooperatives.

The Caja initially took responsibility for social security needs. This function was taken over by *Lagun Aro*, another second degree cooperative, which was created in 1970. It provides a full range of welfare benefits, from child allowances to old-age pensions covering all the workers and their families – 45,000 people in all. Contributions are deducted from member earnings but extra funds are contributed by the cooperatives and the Bank. It also provides health care and monitors industrial safety conditions, but is constrained in providing major medical services by the difficulty of retaining doctors within the narrow pay differentials of the Group.

Expanding the technological base required training and research. *Alecoop*, a cooperative factory *cum* training school was founded in 1966. By 1980 there were 1200 technical students who were able to put themselves through school by working part time in Alecoop, of which they could become full members during their studies. This necessitated the payment of a capital contribution, just as on the adult cooperatives but on a smaller scale. An unusual feature given the local environment is the encouragement of technical training among girls, to avoid the creation of 'a female class of industrial drudges and low-skilled office workers'.[1] Alecoop students elect one-third of the Board of Directors: one third is elected by the permanent staff and one third by the industrial cooperatives. As well as enlarging the pool of trained workers, Alecoop also provides a nucleus of socialized cooperative recruits. *Ikerlan*, a common research and development cooperative was established in 1977 at a cost of some $12 million, to achieve scale economies in this vital area. With a staff of 43 full-time and 18 part-time specialists Ikerlan's mandate is to upgrade the technical capability of the cooperative group to meet that of foreign competition. Japan in particular is seen as a threat to the product lines produced by the group. Among other activities, Ikerlan has designed its own industrial robot, Gizamat.

The expansion of the Group had encouraged a wide range of other cooperative activities. As Mondragon grew from a village to a town of 30,000, property values rose and housing became costly. The group stepped in, and so far has built 14 housing estates, funded by the Caja and run as cooperatives. Consumers are catered to by *Eroski* a second-degree retail cooperative with 650 members and branches all over the Basque country serving one eighth of the Basque population.

After the Civil War Basque and Catalan, the two regional languages, were repressed. To preserve Basque, secret schools were established, one in Mondragon under the guidance of Arizmendi. With Franco's death in November 1975 these schools came into the open and flourished. Many were organized as cooperatives. Parents and the industrial cooperatives which bear much of the cost of schooling are members of the education cooperatives and hence have a large say in the content of education.

During Mondragon's expansion the Group has been consistently profitable. Measures of profitability are provided by Thomas and Logan (1982), Chapter 5. Growth of sales has been impressive; 30 percent annually over the 1960s from a small base, and 8 percent annually over 1970–79. Despite this decrease in the growth rate, the average annual sales increment has been constant during these periods. The individual cooperatives have significant market share in certain products (for selected consumer durables up to 30 percent). But they are not large in terms of Spanish enterprises because of the decision to avoid increasing size beyond 500, the level considered appropriate for cooperative-style management.

Figure 2.1
Typical Organization of a Mondragon Cooperative

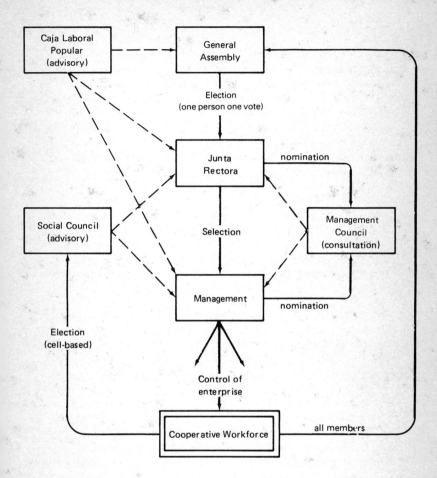

By 1979 the share of exports in total sales had risen to 18 per cent: the export target is 30 per cent of sales by 1985. The emphasis on exports reflects the realization that with the prospect of Spain joining the European Economic Community, the days of relying on the protected home market are limited. The same concern has impelled a move to technical and product upgrading. This has involved steadily increasing capital/man ratios and greater automation. In 1980 fixed capital averaged between $30,000 and $40,000 per worker but was far higher on some of the newer cooperatives. Increased capital intensity appears to have resulted in the cooperatives experiencing rapidly increased labour productivity (despite continued job creation) but in only moderate levels of total factor productivity. The ratio of surplus to gross value added has exceeded that in the local industry by a considerable margin. Profits of the older, larger cooperatives have compensated for the losses of the newer, smaller cooperatives with high ratios of capital/man. Overall, Mondragon has been profitable and appears to have outperformed its capitalist environment by a considerable margin. In common with capitalist industry Mondragon has not gone unscathed by recent economic slowdown. Particularly vulnerable have been the young firms, which have not had the time to fully establish themselves. The Group is heavily concentrated in traditional manufactures which have born the brunt of recession. In fact the ratio of surplus to gross value added fell dramatically from 27 per cent in 1973 to only 6 per cent in 1978 and has recovered little.[2]

Organization and Structure
The formal organizational structure of a typical Mondragon cooperative does not differ too greatly from that of a capitalist corporation. Figure 2.1 depicts the essentials. All cooperateurs are members of the General Assembly which elects a Board of Directors, the *Junta Rectora* on a one-man one-vote basis. The Board in turn selects management. The Social Council is similar to the German or French Works Council. Each cell of ten workers elects a representative to the Social Council which serves in an advisory capacity to management and the Board. The Management Council is an advisory and consultative group which is nominated by management and the Board, and meets at least once a month.

The cooperatives do not formally pay wages, but concede advances out of anticipated profits on a compressed scale. The range of the scale is limited in three dimensions as an important factor to encourage solidarity. Firstly, the base rate of pay is comparable to, or slightly exceeds, that in surrounding industry. Secondly, within individual cooperatives, a 1:3 range was maintained until the late 1970s, although special bonuses to managers could extend this to 1:4.5. The range itself has now been extended to 1:4.5: by 1982 pressure had mounted to widen it to 1:5. Further extension of the range in disposable income results if account is taken of the method of deducting social security contributions, but compression is still tight. While lower grade workers benefit slightly relative to outside comparators, higher grade and managerial cooperateurs receive less than half what they could receive in conventional firms. Thirdly, relativities in average earnings are controlled within narrow bounds between cooperatives according to profitability and social needs.

Containment of earnings is an important part of maintaining solidarity between the Group and surrounding communities. It counters the tendency of worker cooperatives to restrict entry in favour of raising incomes of existing cooperateurs. Without restrictions and with equal sharing, hiring is only justified to existing members if the product of a new entrant exceeds the average product of those on the cooperative. Containment also contributes to job creation by increasing reinvestible surplus and preventing the rundown of capital by cooperateurs with a limited working horizon. Thus, Mondragon's 'open door' policy involves a commitment to provide jobs for the local Basque community and creates strong bonds between the enterprises and their surroundings.

An individual's position on the pay scale is determined by the number of 'points' assigned on the basis of specified criteria. These are: level of qualifications, degree of responsibility, unusually hard or dangerous work and 'social integration'. The weights are not immutably fixed but can vary to reflect changing priorities as perceived by cooperative members. Debate over pay scales has been intense. Disputes over relativities led to the only strike in Mondragon's history, that at Ulgor in 1974. This was a traumatic experience for Mondragon but it was dealt with firmly. Seventeen cooperateurs were expelled and 397 severely penalized after rejecting an ultimatum from the Junta Rectora to return to work. This experience, which was thought to be related to the size of Ulgor (over 3,000 members) played a part in the decision to limit other individual units to around 500 members.

Mondragon rules governing capital and equity are complex. Net profits (or net revenues minus payroll costs, interest and depreciation) are allocated to individual accounts and to two collective accounts, Collective Reserves and the Social Fund, according to a set formula. Individual accounts receive up to 70 per cent of small profits but the proportion allocated to reserves rises as profits increase. The Social Fund receives a flat 10 per cent. The formula is reversed for losses, 70 per cent of which must be borne by individual accounts and 30 per cent by reserves.[3] Individual accounts receive interest at fixed rates and are revalued annually to reflect inflation and changed market conditions. Profit distribution to individuals' accounts is in proportion to their total work and interest incomes not to capital owned, so that long-serving worker members receive larger shares. Distribution is more equal than it would be if made on the basis of capital alone.

Capital contributions are required from workers joining new or existing cooperatives. The amount varies but is equivalent to about one year's pay at the lower levels. On retirement, accumulated profits must by Spanish cooperative law be paid out within two years. Cooperateurs may not sell their shares, and voluntary departures may involve a penalty of up to 30 per cent of accumulated profits, although this is discretionary and imposed only when capital withdrawal is seen as a threat to the enterprise. Individuals are not, therefore, 'tied in' to their cooperatives in practice, but circumstances resulting in waves of departures are likely to result in some blocking of funds. The financial relationships between the individual cooperatives and the Caja Laboral Popular are dealt with by Thomas and Logan (1982).

Although Mondragon's criteria for cooperateur selection appear a little unusual relative to the hiring criteria of firms, this reflects the different roles of cooperateur and worker. In contrast to the emphasis on qualities of obedience and regularity noted in conventional recruitment,[4] Mondragon emphasizes, besides skill and education, variables which measure the degree of integration of workers in their local communities. Following acceptance, a worker undergoes a trial period of six months during which time foremen's reports include assessments of his social acceptability. This screening, and the probable self-selection among potential applicants aware of the criteria for joining the cooperative, serve to identify and reject workers viewing the cooperatives as just another work opportunity and with little 'cooperative' potential. Similar criteria are applied in assessing candidates for advancement within the cooperatives.

Mondragon provides no formal guarantee of lifetime employment. But it is generally accepted that adjustment to structural or market change will not be through job shedding. Cooperateurs may be reallocated between cooperatives which operate a revenue-sharing insurance scheme. They continue to receive 80 per cent of their salary if unavoidably laid off. This, of course, inhibits redundancy since costs of unemployment are so high for the group. Transfers between cooperatives are not unusual. They are also a means for reabsorbing co-operateurs dismissed from managerial positions, a not infrequent event as described below.

Work discipline is closely regulated by rules internal to each cooperative. Misdemeanours are classified as light, grave and very grave. The most frequent offence is bad timekeeping; serious disciplinary problems are rare. Penalties range from written warnings through suspension to losses of income for up to sixty days. Striking against management is still punishable by expulsion. Despite the strong Basque allegiance of the Mondragon group, the anti-strike ethic has not been weakened to accommodate sympathy strikes in favour of Basque nationalism or workers in general. However, to focus on punishment alone is one-sided. An important element of discipline consists of educational seminars to reinforce the ethic of cooperativism among Mondragon's members. Mondragon's ideal is to replace externally imposed discipline by self-discipline. It therefore devotes considerable time and effort to inculcating the cooperative ethic:

> We find it very important to ensure that people who come to join the cooperative are made very aware of what cooperativism is all about, and what the enterprise stands for. To date [Ulgor] has organised 14 courses. We have covered about 800 members so far. The courses last for 92 hours and concern the structure of the firm and reasons for being part of the experience. We also explain the different aspects of production, and cover systems of product development, inventiveness, quality of production, marketing, etc. We also explain social aspects like the capitalist system, the socialist system, and economic history. Then we explain the structure of the actual enterprise: the different departments like personnel, selection, social security, etc. It's a comprehensive course and we don't consider it a waste of money.[5]

The essence of Mondragon is sometimes considered to be its rules and attempts to replicate it have laid great stress on its formal structure at a point in time.[6] It is important to recognize, however, that its rules are only a part of its defining characteristics; perhaps more important has been its ability to learn from experience and adjust its structure to fulfill a consistent set of mainly pragmatic objectives. To create jobs, generate incomes and protect the interests of cooperateurs and their surrounding communities Mondragon acts within normal commercial bounds. It uses and develops the cooperative framework to further these ends.

3 Three Industrial Models: Western, Japanese and Cooperative

Mondragon is a unique worker cooperative. In terms of size, growth, range of production activities and the extent to which it is integrated with local communities it goes far beyond cooperatives typically found in capitalist countries. It is also one of the few enterprises which satisfy rules suggested by Jaroslav Vanek as characteristic of a genuine cooperative.[1] Its emphasis on individual-account shareholding causes it to differ fundamentally from cooperatives organized on the Yugoslav model in which capital is socially owned. From some perspectives Mondragon is a giant and elaborate partnership between cooperateurs and the local community. It is neither capitalist nor socialist but represents a true industrial alternative. Many aspects of its organization diverge from those of capitalist enterprise or traditional partnership. One of the factors causing this divergence is the need to maintain a high degree of consensus within the organization to permit efficient operation of firms with a highly democratic control structure, at least in theory.

It is therefore instructive to compare Mondragon with other consensus-organizations operating in the productive sphere. The Japanese corporations or the Western Z firms are commonly considered to include elements of consensus in their organization. These and stereotypical Western capitalist industry in which the discretionary element is minimized are interesting comparators to Mondragon. In traditional Western industry the employment relationship stresses the cash nexus almost exclusively. On Mondragon, the Japanese corporations and the Z firms an enriched employment relationship is considered crucial for viability. Its commercial value was, however, also seen as key to the establishment of large-scale capitalist firms at the start of the Industrial Revolution. A major protagonist of this view was Robert Owen, one of the earliest and most influential philanthropist–industrialists.

Paternalism and Profit in the Industrial Revolution
From the late eighteenth to the mid nineteenth century England moved

from a predominantly agricultural society to the first industrial nation. This period was characterized by rapid growth of population and industrial output, urban expansion and social upheaval.[2] According to Owen, the moral and social conditions of early factory workers left much to be desired:

> Theft and the receipt of stolen goods was their trade, idleness and drunkenness their habit, falsehood and deception their garb, dissention – civil and religious – their daily practice: they united in a zealous systematic opposition to their employers.[3]

Anomic community relations resulted in conflictual workplace behavior. As is often suggested today in reference to the industrialization of developing countries, economic problems were seen to be essentially social ones:

> children . . . may be formed collectively to have any human character. . . . which, by perseverance under judicious management, may be ultimately moulded into the very image of national wishes and desires.[4]

Thus, Owen set about transforming New Lanark by making it socially responsible, demonstrating wages to be only one factor influencing industrial behaviour. Other factors were associated with the community and included, *inter alia*, home environment, health and education:

> My attention was ever directed to remove . . . much of the immediate causes as were perpetually creating misery among you. . . . I therefore withdrew the most prominent incitements to falsehood, theft, drunkenness and other pernicious habits. . . . and in their stead I introduced other causes, which were intended to produce better external habits.[5]

Owen extended workers' houses, converted liquor stores into good quality foodshops, improved roads, introduced refuse collection and health visitors. New Lanark became 'easiest the cleanest and most sanitary manufacturing town in the country'.[6] Despite severe opposition from his business partners, he instituted a systematic plan for education believing that 'character is formed above all in childhood'. As a result of his efforts he became trusted by workers and was able to secure a high degree of conduct and efficiency which transformed New Lanark into:

> the most successful establishment of the day, in its human as well as its commercial results. . . . Owen was a public character and New Lanark a very celebrated place, visited by travellers from all parts of the world and deputations in search of enlightenment.[7]

As nineteenth century travelers went to New Lanark in search of enlightenment, so today industrialists, policy makers and academics visit Mondragon which has established itself as a model for industrial efficiency and harmonious labor relations. As described in Chapter 2, Arizmendi was inspired by the works and writings of Owen in establishing the rules of Mondragon, although in the long-industrialized Basque provinces the rhythm of industrial life was well established, and the novelty of industry was not a major constraint to productive efficiency. Christian and social responsibility were very much at the heart of Owen's philosophy which also stressed the need for two prerequisites to enable the fulfillment of man: (a) the means of production for adequate wealth for all, and (b) the development of suitable relations of production to produce social happiness and order. In the wake of the Industrial Revolution Owen visualized a world of greatly expanded production potential and the possible directions of its social implications: 'The great importance of our times is that both prerequisites for universal happiness are at hand.'[8]

How might we assess Owen's philosophy in the light of contemporary value systems? He set great store on individual happiness and therefore can be viewed as a Benthamite utilitarian. However, in contrast to many later followers of Bentham he believed that market mechanisms alone would be inadequate to deliver social conditions which he saw as a prerequiste to establishing the appropriate environment for production. While the force of this argument, that 'the market cannot do it all' may have been diminished in the richer countries by improved living standards, it still remains a crucial one in developing countries. Disease, malnutrition and illiteracy contribute significantly to their low productivity.[9] Owen held great faith in education and self-improvement as means to enlightenment. He set out to 'remoralize the lower order' both out of altruism and from conviction that this could be commercially profitable. Most advocates of employee ownership and worker cooperatives, including those at Mondragon, similarly claim converging rather than competing goals in commercial profitability and social objectives. So do supporters of the Z firms.

Owen acknowledged that reform might not be self supporting initially. He depended for funds on sources concerned with a combination of social and economic priorities as did Arizmendi when starting his own training school and establishing the first cooperative in Mondragon. Owen's patrons' desire that the New Lanark experiment should be profitable limited his involvement in social and welfare activities. This was perhaps fortunate, since he seemed to be most successful precisely when constrained to the sphere of production and began to falter after broadening his scope. A successful paternalist capitalist, Owen failed at Utopian socialism. By 1916 New Lanark was highly profitable[10] and had become '. . . the largest cotton undertaking, measured by numbers employed in Britain. . . . wages were low by comparison with other mills, but were apparently acceptable because of the superior social welfare benefits.'[11]

The benefits provided by Owen seem commonplace today. But he also initiated sophisticated means of social control and succeeded in the task despaired of by other capitalist employers in the early stages of the Industrial Revolution: to accommodate good behavior to factory life. His community-oriented welfare approach rested on a fundamental tradeoff: the inculcation of an ideology of work in return for support against the misery and hardship of poverty and unemployment. The experiment of New Lanark was institutionalized to 'meet the same difficulties of labour discipline and the adoption of the unruly Scottish labourers to new industrial work patterns.'[12] Owen was later to apply his principles in New Hampshire across the Atlantic, in New Harmony (1824–30).

How did Owen's views appear to the Left? As they opposed both individualistic utilitarianism associated with pure meritocracy and the aristocratic tenet of innate superiority, they were not popular with the establishment. However, with great faith in the role of rational behaviour, approving utopian ideals and believing in the need to secure social consensus, he rejected class conflict as a means to an end. In no sense can Owenite paternalism be radical. Thus, he was denegrated by Marx and Engels, although the latter found some words of praise for him. Owen came progressively to resent the appropriation of surplus by capital, from conviction that individuals had a moral right to derive utility from the proceeds of their own labor. He also concurred with Marx in seeing the progressive immizerisation of the working class as the natural course of capitalist development and envisaging a consequent tendency to underconsumption. But Owen firmly believed that by planning and rational action within capitalism these trends could be overcome without resorting to revolution. Neither Owen's reformism nor worker cooperatives have found favour with the Left.

Owen's brand of paternalism emphasized changing the environment as a source of increased productivity within the firm. Because of its emphasis on the role of society, it may be considered as 'social paternalism', which is distinguished from later 'industrial paternalism'. As discussed in more detail below, the latter emphasizes the role of paternalism in overcoming *internal*, firm-specific organizational obstacles to productive efficiency. All forms of paternalism came to be eclipsed in the rapid growth of the capitalist economy from the mid 19th century onwards. Firms insulated themselves from their social surroundings as far as they could, and adopted the principles later codified by Taylor into scientific management. So extensively has scientific management permeated the philosophy and administration of Western work-organization that only since the 1950s have its premises begun to be seriously questioned.

Scientific Management: A Reappraisal

How far the rise of scientific management in the Western industrial economies was (a) predetermined by the *technical* requirements of production, (b) impelled by the rapid *growth* of industry or (c) consciously *chosen* out of a range of possible alternatives to limit the power of individual workers hence control the working classes, is still debated.[13] The deterministic versus voluntaristic nature of the roots of scientific management is important in assessing the prospective viability of cooperatives. Do market forces impose a particular internal management style? Can alternative sytems of industrial organization compete with conventional Western firms? Until the emergence of Japanese industrial power, the rise to prominence of scientific management was commonly viewed as inevitable, but there is now a body of evidence supporting the third option, that of deliberate choice.

What are the main characteristics of scientific management style? The most important features are two: separating planning from doing and reaping the benefits of intense specialization. The first involves defining two broad categories of jobs. Planning is the responsibility of a small group of owners or trusted employees loyal to the objectives of capital. These should identify with the firm and feel responsible for its success. In contrast to this group which operates with a wide range of discretion, the mass of workers is expected to execute simple, easily monitored tasks which are to be standardized and routinized as much as possible to separate the attributes of the job from those of the worker. This renders workers interchangeable and facilitates the disciplinary sanction of 'hire and fire' policy because firing is less costly to the firm. Threat of dismissal replaces any loyalty or attachment to the goals of the enterprise as an incentivating force. With little presumed loyalty, the tasks of the mass of workers must be performed with little discretion.

'Low trust' hierarchical relationships between upper and lower grades of employees, and antagonistic rather than cooperative patterns of labor relations are therefore a presumed norm for the scientifically managed firm. Individual firms within this general type of enterprise may do far better. But there are strong tendencies towards the emergence of adversarial attitudes. Job fragmentation (needed for control) works against the education of employees who lack skills sufficiently general to envisage an upwardly mobile career within the firm: crossing the divide between the two groups is difficult. The presumed short-term nature of the employment contract leaves an instantaneous cash nexus – the wage – as the central, indeed the only, feature of the employment relationship. Employees outside the small group of trusted managers cannot sensibly be rewarded even with stock options given the hire and fire policy. Even if they were, their presumed lack of discretion would result in little advantage to the firm from such incentives. Widespread resort to bonuses and other incentive payments within the scientifically managed firm is actually an admission of failure – an acknowledgement that the system of monitoring and control is imperfect – and calls into question the foundations of the management philosophy.

Scientific management practices evolved gradually as the prerogatives of a segment of the working class – the foreman – were slowly eroded. In the early 19th century firms and factories were small. Even large enterprises typically consisted of only a few hundred employees. Within these units, foremen had considerable autonomy. Their range of discretion extended over the organization of work and the recruiting of production teams. At its extreme, the early industrial factory can be considered as a set of subcontracting arrangements (sometimes) gathered under one roof.

This system increasingly came to be seen as inefficient, particularly in the US with rapid growth of the industrial labor force and of individual factories. The American industrial experience involved the absorption of successive waves of ethnically diverse immigrants, many unaccustomed to factory life. This enabled the prerogatives of already-established workers to be undercut and heightened the premium on techniques of mass control which were independent of specific cultural norms. At the same time, competition between successive ethnic groups inhibited the growth of class-based opposition to the new system of control. Standardization, routinization and de-skilling became the means of assimilating the new arrivals into the expanding American industrial environment (Braverman 1974). Scientific management was adopted more slowly in other industrial countries such as Britain, where the economic environment did not place a premium on innovative behavior (Hobsbawm 1968). This was because of sheltered markets, cheap raw materials, little wage pressure (Hill 1982) and less cultural diversity. The need was less pressing and indifference on the part of class-based capital to applied science and technology (Levine 1967) heightened resistance to its introduction.

From the present perspective several features of scientific management are particularly important:

(a) separation of the attributes of the job from those of the worker results in short-term employment contracts;

(b) firms and communities are therefore distinct. Mobile industry can 'hire and fire' communities as it does workers, by changing location;

(c) labour mobility may result in a substantial disincentive to firms educating and training workers especially when acquired skills are transferable to competitors;

(d) the complexity of programs of social involvement with local communities and within the firm preclude their introduction in the fluid labour environment;

(e) sophisticated monitoring systems render high-trust relationships unnecessary;

(f) because of low trust and lack of information (partly a consequence of specialization) labour cannot be expected to accept remuneration in forms related to the profitability of the enterprise;

(g) the same factors cause labour relations to follow an asymmetric-information game structure characterized by strikes and industrial disruption. Labor has only one way of determining the firm's willingness and ability to pay, by threatening to withdraw from the production process, so testing the resolution of capital.

In a democratic political system successful scientific management leads inevitably to political curbs on the prerogatives of capital because of the nature of this bargaining process. This occurs even when capitalism is not ideologically challenged. The more successful are management techniques the less leverage has labor to affect the outcome of negotiation. Even if a particular wage settlement is not so low as to yield excessive profits, labour has no way of assessing this, and less reason to trust management. The information problem is further complicated when multinational enterprise is considered. It is hard to separate out the actual profitability of a particular plant given the ability to shift profits through arbitrary accounting prices. The only way for labor to regain power through collective bargaining is to limit the 'hire and fire' power of capital and to improve access to company information. In all Western economies labor's struggle at national (and sometimes international) levels has had an impact on the environment external to individual enterprises and, through legislation, has conditioned the internal process of negotiations.[14]

Taylor, the foremost codifier of scientific management, was a practicing manager and consultant rather than a social theorist. He viewed its techniques as methods to increase economic growth through raising productivity rather than tools to subjugate the working classes and redistribute *existing* income towards capital. Increased wage payments, made possible by a more efficient specialized productive system would offset any tendency to resist its principles. Taylor thus foreshadowed the 'end of ideology' debate of the 1950s and 1960s (Bell

1962). During this period, empirical study suggested that rapid growth and economism were tending to undercut any notion of the working class as an ideological opposition to capitalism. This proposition stood in direct contrast to Marxist predictions of an increasingly impoverished, alienated and class-conscious proletariat. It was not claimed that growth made workers fervent supporters of the system. Studies such as Goldthorpe, *et al.* (1968) which focused on the process of neutralizing the oppositional role of labor suggested that workers instead became 'privatised'. They would divert their attention from the class struggle, towards acquiring and caring for private commodities for their own consumption. These studies have been interpreted by others (McKenzie and Silver 1968) as also suggesting that a considerable degree of social criticism coexisted with the resulting social apathy. The cash nexus which secures labor's compliance with prospering capitalism may also be seen as a source of potential instability in the event that capitalist growth slows (Westergaard 1970; Moorhouse 1976) because all nonpecuniary links binding workers to the social system have been undercut. But Taylor's assessment of labor's response to the tradeoff between material reward and loss of discretionary power has been broadly validated by the experience of the major industrialized countries, and most clearly so in the United States. Materialism has undercut militancy.

To some extent the formalization of scientific management into a doctrine of productive efficiency has helped to produce this response. Its philosophy – that managers are legitimized through their necessary role in production and entitled to superior financial rewards and capitalist-class privileges – has played a large role in sustaining capitalist ideology through the period of divorce between ownership and control (Nichols 1969). Much as a raw army recruit may be persuaded that strict military discipline offers him the best chance of survival in actual warfare, so Taylorism invokes strong material sanctions against disruption of the industrial order.

Technocratic control within firms may not have been out of line with the prevailing socio-political environments in the main industrialized countries at the turn of the century. Politically powerful labor movements were less prominent and the aspirations of the great mass were limited for want of access to higher education which was still the province of the privileged few. Agriculture still provided a large potential reserve army of labor. The *laissez-faire* capitalist ethic was widely accepted, and Western societies were yet to face the profound changes stemming from two World Wars.

Several factors led, in the postwar period, to the challenging of scientific management theory. The first articulated challenge came in the form of Elton Mayo's Hawthorne experiments of the 1950s which were to form the basis of the Human Relations School of Management. As suggested by its name, this attempted a more integrated and holistic system of industrial organization. Following on from the Mayo experiments, the 1960s saw increasing experimentation with alternative techniques of motivation and control which attempted to modify the adverse effects of Taylorism. The success of German industry and 'codetermination' became apparent in the 1960s. As growth slowed in the 1970s, the dynamism of Japanese industry which also emphasized consensus became apparent. At the start of the 1980s the search for alternatives has intensified.

As noted above, the main underlying development causing scientific management to be questioned has been an increasing reluctance to accept its principles in the Western market economies. This proposition is difficult to define precisely and test. The contrast between the behavioral model of an individual within the scientifically managed firm and that within democratic society at large is quite apparent. The philosophy of production accords most workers the status of robots, to be used as efficiently as possible accepting all regulation without question. Outside the firm, the same workers are required to exercise their individual and collective judgements on the laws governing a society which includes their own firm. Were material rewards the only concern, reconciliation of this conflict is easier if one accepts the Taylorist efficiency arguments for scientific management. But even this would require a complex system of side-payments to ensure that individuals received the benefit of improvements in efficiency which otherwise they might be induced to block. The Owenite tradeoff – work discipline in return for material security – is less pressing after an unprecedented spell of economic growth and blunted by the widespread introduction of social security systems. It is no coincidence that some of the widely publicized attempts to break with the work fragmentation of scientific management originated in Sweden, which has long been characterized by extensive unionization (at 80 per cent the highest in Europe, Hill 1981), advanced and widespread education, extensive social security and limits on the immigration of unskilled workers. The Volvo Kalma experiment (Aguren 1976), despite being localized and concentrating on reform of only part of the apparatus of scientific management, is famed for the extent to which production processes of a supposedly technically rigid kind were rearranged to accommodate a new system of work organization. This was not done for greater efficiency in the narrow sense. The new technology involving working groups rather than assembly lines was seen as more compatible with a desire for discretion and variety in work. It was hoped that productivity would rise due to the diminution of frustration, industrial deviance and strikes.

Most of the industrial countries have introduced legislation aimed at limiting the prerogatives of management and hence of capital. This may be interpreted as an attempt to restructure intra-firm relationships to be more compatible with those of society. The trend to regulation has been less marked in the US than in Europe and Britain; see Leveson and Wheeler (1980), but reflects a common underlying shift in political power and the evolution of social preference. In some views this trend is seen as a serious threat to increased productivity under existing management systems: Nelson (1980), Ohlin (1980); and others not willing to attribute a major part of past productivity declines to social restraints acknowledge that improved social arrangements of production may need to play a major role in regaining momentum (Thurow 1981).

A second feature leading scientific management to be challenged is the increased role of human capital in production. This places labor and (physical) capital in a somewhat more symmetric position, each dependent on a third factor – skills embodied in people – which cannot be depersonalized. To realize the benefits of technical deepening requires more complex organizations with an increasing component of high-level white collar workers. The dominance of the technology factor in leading industries of the richer countries has been demonstrated in a number of studies of comparative advantage, Hufbauer (1970), Aho and Orr (1980). While the leading sectors in the advanced countries may be little more physical capital-intensive than the more traditional, contracting, usually import-competing sectors they are invariably more intensive in research and development spending and in human capital. Employees in these sectors are more highly educated on average, and, in the United States at least, are known to include a smaller fraction of minority groups.

Human capital intensity undermines traditional control methods. Scientific management has been applied to lower clerical grades but, because of the difficulty of measuring the productivity of service occupations and the impossibility of fragmenting and de-skilling many service tasks, has yet to be applied consistently in service sectors. Greater dependence on human capital introduced crucial quasi-service characteristics into industry. It blurs the distinction between planning and doing and decreases the scope of traditional monitoring.

This might matter little if higher-level employees were automatically socialized into the capitalist class. However, as shown by Goldthorpe *et al.* (1968) for Britain, it has been necessary to recruit members of the capitalist technocracy from a wide variety of class backgrounds (although the 'inner core' of top capitalists appear to be more class-stable: Miliband 1969). Upper white collar employees could not therefore be assumed to inherit the attitudes and ethics of highly trusted management but were more difficult to control than blue collar workers. Together with legislative and social change this has led to increased interest in incentives and attempts to overcome the adversarial labor relations characteristic of scientific management.

Japan: a Model for the 1980s?

As analyzed by Dore (1973) and Marsh and Mannari (1976) the factor common to firms operating in the 'privileged third' of the Japanese economy is an enriched employment relationship extending far beyond the cash nexus. The elaborate system of reciprocal firm–employee rights and obligations is sometimes referred to as the 'paternalism–lifetime–commitment model'. By any standards Japan's economic growth after the Second World War has been high and the performance of its industry spectacular. Labor productivity has risen rapidly as has total factor productivity, and by the early 1970s Japanese technology was considered to be on a par with that of the United States (Jorgensen and Nishimizu 1978). Not only did Japanese products penetrate foreign markets but Japan speedily acquired a reputation for product excellence and reliability. It has also succeeded in adjusting its export mix to reflect its technological comparative advantage over emerging lower wage competitors such as Korea and Taiwan.

How can so outstanding a record be explained? At national level a variety of explanations has been advanced, emphasizing political, socio-cultural, psychological and other factors (see Marsh and Mannari 1976, Morishima 1982 for discussion). But at least a part of Japanese success is generally ascribed to factors internal to major firms, notably their distinctive pattern of industrial organization. To what extent this itself is a consequence of national characteristics is still debated but, as in the case of scientific management, evidence exists to suggest that the 'paternalism–lifetime–commitment model' arises to some extent out of choice and may be applicable over a range of cultures and societies.

In contrast to the ideals of scientific management, the 'paternalist–lifetime–commitment' system seeks to integrate employees into their companies, and to shift their allegiance from lateral, class-based identification towards alignment with a production unit spanning a range of occupations. If such a high-trust relationship can be established and maintained, extreme monitoring of performance is less necessary, although many of the methods developed to assist scientific management are carried over as planning tools. Job fragmentation therefore loses one source of appeal to management (controllability) and need not be pushed beyond the level optimal for production efficiency to reduce worker power. In fact, fragmentation is liable to be less than this 'optimal' level with greater emphasis on generalist skills and group responsibility because varied work has three advantages. Firstly, it reduces job monotony hence is less liable to lead to an alienated workforce. Secondly, it is important that employees gain an insight into the organization as a whole, to foster integration. Thirdly, job rotation is needed to maintain labor flexibility given constraints on hiring and firing and to permit employees to acquire a range of skills sufficient to build a career in the enterprise.

High-trust relationships require the prospect of long-term employment. Employees cannot trust management if they feel that they are the first to shoulder the burden of recession through job loss. A long-term perspective is also needed to prevent trusted employees from seeking short-term gains at the expense of the long-run interests of the firm. This raises the problem of consensus-preserving pay and seniority scales which at the same time are consistent with efficiency. Promotion is typically slower and more uniform than in scientifically managed firms with pay scales related to seniority (age, length of service) rather than to immediate responsibility. Substantial responsibility may be placed on the shoulders of relatively junior staff who are rewarded with an implicit promise that they will profit by their efforts, but only in the longer run.

From the perspective of management, this system has advantages and drawbacks. On the one hand, the climate of labor relations may be more favorable than that in many scientifically managed firms. Management usually has to deal only with company unionism and should encounter a relatively constructive attitude among the workforce. Managers also avoid the disruption of the many transfers between organizations which they usually need under scientific management to further their careers, and may be subjected to less intensive stress if the current financial 'bottom line' is felt to be a less pressing imperative relative to future goals. On the other hand, the management task is more complex in other dimensions, since the key to profitability is seen to involve both the *objective* factors faced by the firm – markets and technology – and the *subjective* consciousness of its workforce which needs to maintain cohesion and trust. Some of the institutions developed to further solidarity and to tap the collective wisdom of the firm, such as the quality circle, place a strain on lower and middle management whose role is challenged by the involvement of lower-rank workers in the planning process.

Ironically, the development of this pattern of industrial relations owes much to two American consultants, Deming and Juran, who were influential during the early years of postwar reconstruction. At this time it was not clear whether scientific management or the lifetime–paternalist model would dominate Japanese labor relations. Although the latter may have been seen as more compatible with the social environment, its adoption was by no means inevitable. This view gains credence from the existence of capitalist firms organized along similar lines in the Western economies, against the general trend. These Z firms described by Ouchi (1982) include such national leaders as Hewlett Packard, Eastman Kodak and IBM. Their commercial success suggests that the limits set by technology are sufficiently broad to enable consensus-type industrial enterprises to exist in a wide class of cultures through universal principles.

The Z firms depart from conventional Western archetypes (the so-called 'A firms') in the Japanese direction rather than duplicate faithfully all aspects of Japanese management style. They stem from an independent paternalist tradition, with ethical, rather than direct historical links to early Western paternalism. Often the Z firms started in small towns, which inculcated a sense of social responsibility and relationship with the community. They may invariably be traced to founders with strong ethical values who then transplanted these into their organizations. A key element of these systems is to justify financial success. Profits are justified mainly because they are necessary to achieve other objectives notably growth, employment and service to clients. Commercial success is not seen as inherently worthy in its own right but is legitimized as an instrument to achieve loftier aims.

Despite their similarities, the Z firms and their Japanese counterparts diverge in some respects which reflect their vastly differing institutional environments. In particular entry procedures differ. The major Japanese firms select almost automatically from specified and prestigious schools. These derive their status from their links with the firm and are enabled to screen entrants in intensely competitive examinations: entry to top Japanese companies is decided as early as kindergarten stage in an even earlier round of competition. The Z firms conform to normal selection procedures at point-of-entry, much like their A firm counterparts. Whereas the selection procedures of the latter tend to be individualistic and narrowly job-related, it may be that other criteria are applied by the Z firms as well. They have been observed to possess more homogeneous workforces than the A firms, although they are undoubtedly less homogeneous than Japanese corporations because of their relatively heterogeneous environment and the absence of pre-selection forces towards conformism. Socio-cultural homogeneity almost surely eases the task of sustaining consensus and creating a sense of group identity, so that selection criteria taking this into account may not be irrational for the Z firms. Similarly, compromises between Japanese and Western reward systems and low labour turnover rather than lifetime employment characterize the Z firms.

Both the Japanese corporations and the Z firm grant significant managerial prerogatives to non-managerial employees through formalized arrangements such as working groups. Increasingly, these have begun to be implemented in A firms also, although the industrial relations environment in the latter is less favourable to such efforts. As analyzed by Bradley and Hill (1983), these groups, when properly constituted, are carefully structured to encourage cross-disciplinary interaction, involving employees with a variety of skills from different departments. This has been found necessary to reduce opposition to suggestions for change which cut across departmental lines, and to avoid too narrow a group perspective. Quality circles are therefore very different from worker groups drawn, for purposes of representation, from individual working sections.

Organizational Characteristics in Three Industrial Models

Having reviewed the Western and Japanese industrial models, we are now in a position to compare these with the Mondragon group, which differs most fundamentally from both in its structure of ownership. How different is Mondragon in other dimensions: the employment relationship, accountability of management and the system of rewards? To assess differences and similarities, Table 3.1 lists 16 characteristics, and the extent to which these are typically associated with the three organizational forms.

The first three characteristics cover enterprise and group structure, the selection and accountability of management and relationships between the firm and local community. The autonomy of individual cooperatives renders the Mondragon group distinctive, in terms of group structure, relative to the other corporate forms. In some respects it comes closer to the Japanese corporations with a financial institution at the center and an absence of 'arms-length' sources of loan capital. While the selection of managers is not too different on Mondragon, their ultimate responsibility to their worker–shareholders is indeed unusual. Mondragon, finally, resembles the Japanese model far more closely than the Western firm in its involvement in the community but the concept of 'community' is wider. It extends beyond the immediate families of workers to include the local population.

The next eight characteristics cover mainly non-wage aspects of the employment relationship; the last five mainly the determination of earnings. Like the A firms and Z firms (but not the Japanese)

Table 3.1 A comparison of organizational characteristics

Organizational characteristic	Western corporation 'A firm'	Japanese corporation 'Z firm'	Mondragon group
1. Group Structure	Corporate headquarters with control, or isolated firms. Typically little management involvement of sources of loan finance (except some European countries notably Germany).	Major financial institution with corporate control at center of manufacturing group. 'Outside' lenders not prominent.	Cooperative credit union (Caja Laboral Popular) at center of cooperative group. Financial control, provision of technical and managerial advice. Ultimate autonomy lies with individual cooperatives.
2. Management Selection and Accountability	Selected by Board of Directors and top management, accountable to shareholders through Board elected by shareholders.	Selected by Board and top management, accountable to 'the corporation' and ultimately to shareholders (largely Banks) through corporate responsibility.	Selected by top management, accountable to General Assembly of works through Board of Directors nominated by the (elected) General Assembly. Prime responsibility to plant and its workers, not group.
3. Community and Firm Relationships	Separated deliberately. Where links are close, this is typically for spatial reasons (company towns).	Paternalistic fostering of firm-oriented community. Company identity, family holidays, company housing, etc.	Deliberate reciprocal involvement, directed towards providing jobs and education for Basque community, plus a range of services.
4. Selection of Members of Enterprise	Criteria applied at point of entry, mainly individualistic (skills, past record, etc.), plus some attention to willingness to accept discipline.	Prescriptive–competitive entry as far back as kindergarten into 'company schools' early establishment of reciprocal obligation of company and individual. In Z firms, selection at point of entry, more emphasis on 'integrative' criteria.	Criteria applied at point of entry. Partly individualistic (skills), largely community-related, and ethnic (assimilation with Basque community is an important attribute.)
5. The Implicit Employment Bargain	Revocable wage contract. Heavy reliance on external labour market, attempts to minimize the role of the internal labour market.	Lifetime employment in custom and practice, modified through early retirement, voluntary days off as necessary, redeployment and subcontracting. Internal labor market emphasized.	Lifetime employment expected. Some redeployment between cooperatives but no layoffs to date. Little use of casual labor, and no buffer through subcontracting. Internal labor market emphasis.
6. Human Capital Development	Some bias against training because of short term employment but specialized training given to employees as required.	Broad skill development encompasses a range of technical aspects and serves an integrative function as well, with emphasis on firm ideology.	Socialization into a particular firm ideology (cooperativism), plus acquisition of specific technical skills.
7. Functional Specialization at Work	Extreme. Blue collar work reduced to simple repetitive tasks to enable easy worker replacement. Extreme management specialization.	Less specialized. Deliberate attempt to limit specialization through matrix management, job rotation and group responsibility.	Work organization does not differ greatly from surrounding firms. There is interest in job enrichment but this is not a prime focus.

8.	Quality Circles/Group Work	Used to limited extent for limited objectives only. Sometimes introduced by management to cut production costs.	Widespread. Structured to cut across functional specializations, and address a wide range of social and technical matters.	Now working group cell organization mainly for representation purposes through the Social Council.
9.	Labour Flexibility within the Enterprise	Specialization limits flexibility. Trade unions constrain flexibility in proportion to their strength.	Labor reallocated between plants and occupations, with approval of labor representatives, both to cope with demand fluctuations and enrich careers.	Workers can be reallocated among cooperatives to cope with demand fluctuations.
10.	Social Benefits During Employment	Varies: company-specific arrangements to cover medical care but public benefits dominate. (Frequently, company and employees split cost of subscription to private health insurance.)	Comprehensive coverage by company, complements limited public benefits in Japan.	Comprehensive coverage by group (Lagun Aro) complements limited public benefits. Cooperateurs outside Spanish Social Security.
11.	Benefits at Retirement	State Social Security System complemented by firm pension plans which pay out only to a limited proportion of employees.	Lump sum payment, based on salary and length of service plus placement in subsidiary firms in Japan.	Cooperative social security and pension plan (currently 60% of final pay) plus payment of accumulated equity (may be around $50,000).
12.	Collective Bargaining	Mixture of economy-wide unions and union-surrogates (US 20%, UK 50%, Sweden 80% union density).	Company unions negotiate terms of collective bargaining.	Broad parameters set by overall group rules. Within these, members set company income policy at plant-level General Assemblies. Grievances and disciplinary aspects channeled through social councils.
13.	Relationship between Responsibility and Pay	Close relationship which can be affected by collective bargaining.	Less close relationship: promotion (in terms of responsibilities) may diverge from pay (set by seniority).	Close relationship within narrow differentials range (see below). All jobs graded on Group scale, rankings determined by individual cooperatives.
14.	Potentially Rapid Increase in Compensation	Yes, with rapid promotion.	No: Pay related largely to length of services, seniority.	Yes, within narrow bounds.
15.	Pay Differentials	Wide: seen as major incentive.	Wide: major reward to seniority and management.	Limited by Group rules. Maximum spread until 1980 of 1:3 subsequently increased to 1:4.5. Lowest pay slightly above Spanish comparators: highest around half of comparator level.
16.	Dependence of pay on profitability	Small, except for marginal rewards to management (such as stock options), and possible job loss. May have involuntary accommodation of rewards to profitability through impact on collective bargaining.	Annual bonuses based on profitability equivalent to around 2 months' salary.	Surplus based on profitability distributed mainly to individual accounts in proportion to labor and interest income.

Mondragon screens and selects at the point of entry, but unlike the A firms the cooperatives place a heavy emphasis on social criteria, to assist integration and promote a homogeneous organization. Mondragon similarly resembles consensus organizations in the lifetime nature of the (presumed) employment contract. As in Japan, internal labor flexibility is needed to permit full employment. Japanese corporations use subcontracting as a buffer, and throw the burden of market fluctuations onto smaller, less formal enterprises. Mondragon does not, hence it lacks even an indirect 'hire and fire' policy. As in Japan, Mondragon emphasizes the upgrading of technical skills and socialization into a specific ideology.

Although Mondragon resembles the Japanese model in adjusting to market changes through internal labor flexibility, there is an interesting difference when it comes to functional specialization. Work organization differs little between Mondragon and its surrounding capitalist firms, and there appear to be no formalized mechanisms, such as quality circles, for tapping the technical expertise of its workers as a management strategy. Cells of the Social Council organized around working groups perform a similar representational function to enterprise unions. Mondragon management is aware of participatory mechanisms and of initiatives to adapt production technology such as that at Kalma. It is highly supportive of such experiments but has not attempted to replicate them. At first sight this might appear unexpected. But apart from possible technical advantages there is less incentive for such experiments in Mondragon. Worker ownership provides an alternative means to generate consensus and integrate the workforce.[15]

Company pension plans in the US (and certain other countries) typically pay out benefits to only a small proportion of long-serving employees. Large Japanese corporations and Mondragon are more generous. The former provide a lump sum payment and frequently place retiring employees in smaller firms, often subsidiaries manufacturing sub-components for their original employers. Their accumulated equity renders Mondragon workers perhaps the best-provided-for of all retirees. For a typical employee this may be in the region of $55,000 (in 1982 prices), plus a pension. Although originally optimistically set to permit retirement on full pay, pension rights were scaled down to 60 per cent of final pay in 1976 as the projected burden of payments became apparent.

The collective bargaining arrangements in Mondragon are distinctive because of the collective role of members in setting pay relativities within individual plants, and their role in specifying and administering disciplinary rules. Within the narrow differentials, promotion can be rapid in Mondragon. This contrasts with the Japanese model where pay differentials are, however, wide. The rapidity of promotion in Mondragon is partly due to the compressed earnings scale. As the cooperatives face difficulty in recruiting experienced managers, they promote rapidly, enriching the jobs of potential managers to provide an incentive for them to remain with the group.

Because of the policy of limiting wage differentials, Mondragon has not found it necessary to separate seniority and pay from responsibility so as to preserve consensus. This has been necessary in other consensus organizations to reduce disruption caused by rapid jumps by individuals in the hierarchy. Within a narrow range, there is a close correspondence between skills, responsibility and other job-related attributes on the one hand and pay on the other.

Finally in Mondragon, the distribution to individual accounts of surpluses based on profitability resembles the payment of bonuses in Japanese firms, except that surplus distribution is a capital rather than a current transaction. Individual accounts bear most of the fluctuation in profitability under Mondragon rules so that the links between profits and incentives is assured. But unlike bonuses, individual accumulated profits cannot be withdrawn until retirement. This renders them closer to stock options to be exercised in the future. In countries where capital markets are not sufficiently developed to allow small investors to hold equity such an option could be an especially attractive incentive. On Mondragon and in Japanese firms, labor routinely accepts a proportion of risk in the form of variable compensation in exchange for greater job security. Collective bargaining in the Western economies has not traditionally accepted this tradeoff. Under extreme duress it has sometimes been directed to a similar end particularly from the start of the 1980s, but is slow to respond and does not always take into account the profitability of individual firms. With slower pay adjustment, employment fluctuations have to bear a greater share of the burden.

Overall, Mondragon appears to resemble the Japanese model in some seven out of sixteen characteristics. In three it comes closer to the A firm model. In the remaining six Mondragon is either distinctive or intermediate.[16] Mondragon therefore shares a number of factors with other consensus-oriented production units and resembles these to a greater extent than it does traditional Western firms. However, it is notable for the methods used to maintain consensus, which are closely related to its unusual pattern of ownership and control.

4 Background to an Analysis

For an industrialized region the Basque country around Mondragon is unusual. It is overwhelmingly rural, with a lack of infrastructure. Inadequate transport, winding single-lane roads through congested villages and its mountainous nature lend the main centers of co-operative activity a somewhat isolated air. Poor communications are a constant complaint at Mondragon, where centralized Spanish policy is seen as unresponsive to local needs. There are few visitors from outside, and few hotels. Signposts with Spanish names are whited-out through Basque nationalist activity and Basque directions (which bear no linguistic relationship to their Spanish equivalents) superimposed. Yet in the valleys modern factories carry out their business competitively, over a wide range of manufacturing activity.

Geography's role is evident in comparing the Basques with the Catalans, the other large cultural minority group within Spain. Catalonia has stood at the crossroads of a variety of cultures – French, Greek, Arab, Roman, Castilian, and has absorbed eclectically from all. The Basque country on the other hand has been bypassed. The immigration of workers from poorer regions of Southern Spain and the struggle against the Franco government and its repression, have increased political reserve and perhaps actually strengthened the resolve to maintain Basque culture.

The Mondragon group is scattered over the Basque provinces. Distances are physically small, but substantial in terms of time and communication. The nucleus is in the town of Mondragon itself, but other cooperatives are dotted through rural areas with some in major industrial centers such as Bilbao, San Sebastian and Vitoria. Logistical difficulties, Basque reserve and political suspicion combine to inhibit data collection, despite the willingness of many individuals to provide information and assistance and the cooperation of the Mondragon group itself.

There were two options for collecting subjective data, open-ended in-depth interviewing of cooperateurs, and more tightly formulated questions able to be put in multiple choice form. Each presents problems of execution and interpretation. Data collection on a large scale proceeded using the second method, but was complemented by in-depth interviewing of a number of key personnel.[1] These included founding cooperateurs, senior management of the Caja Laboral Popular and several cooperatives and of control firms (see below). Statistical material relating to profitability, sales and similar variables was not collected because of its availability in other publications. The record outlined in Chapter 2 explains our *a priori* decision to regard the cooperatives as successful business enterprises.

Two questionnaires were distributed, the second including the possibility of postal return to reduce bias caused by the inclusion of potentially sensitive questions. The surveys were not identical but contained many questions in common. Responses were obtained from a diverse range of cooperatives to reflect variations within the group over size, age, product, technology and location in large and small towns. Overall 1080 replies were achieved, a response rate of 30 per cent of surveyed individuals. The distribution of responses over the various cooperatives is given in Table 4.1. Interviews with cooperateurs emphasized personnel and other policies of the manufacturing cooperatives, firm–community relations and the operation of the Caja.

Mondragon's product and spatial diversity pose some problems for the selection of an appropriate control group. In addition to the normal comparisons of control and subject groups, we decided to use the control to obtain information on perceptions of Mondragon through the eyes of other workers in the Basque country. This was considered useful because Mondragon cooperateurs are partly self-selecting, and because, with long and stable work histories of employment in one enterprise, their assessment of the cooperatives relative to firms outside might be suspect. Some familiarity with Mondragon, even by reputation, was thus essential.[2] Two firms were chosen: Union Carrejera was the major employer in Mondragon before the cooperative movement became established and is comparable to Ulgor. Mayc in Vitoria is located in a large industrial area and in product and technology is comparable with local cooperatives. Obtaining the cooperation of trade unions in the comparator firms proved to be more difficult than persuading management to permit the surveys. Overall, 280 responses were achieved.

The first survey covered eleven cooperatives, concentrating on Ulgor and Arrasate in Mondragon. Newer, smaller enterprises were also surveyed. The second survey covered four cooperatives, two located in the town of Mondragon and two outside, 'n large industrial centers.

Table 4.1 Sampling of cooperatives

Cooperative	Founding date	No. of cooperateurs	Product	Town/Province	Sample size
Ulgor	1956	3,600	Kitchen equipment	Mondragon, Guipuzcoa	298
Irizar	1965	334	Appliances	Ormaiztegui, Guipuzcoa	149
Urssa	1961	276	Construction	Vitoria, Alava	116
Funcor	1955	226	Machine tools	Elorrio, Vizcaya	101
Fagor	1966	573	Domestic electrical goods	Onate, Guipuzcoa	86
Arrasate	1957	500	Machine tools	Mondragon, Guipuzcoa	80
Matrice	1963	240	Metal-stamping	Zamudio, Vizcaya	52
Danona	1962	400	Furniture	Azpeita, Guipuzcoa	32
Orbea	1969	180	Bicycles	Mallabia, Vizcaya	27
Maier	1973	68	Electrical components	Guernica, Guipuzcoa	27
Amat	1963	370	Pipe fittings	Mondragon, Guipuzcoa	21
Lealde	1974	35	Lathes	Lequeito, Vizcaya	20
Tolsan	1957	130	Industrial piping	Amorebeita, Vizcaya	19
Eika	1973	70	Electrical components	St. Andres de Echeverria, Vizcaya	5
Doiki	1972	39	Precision instruments	Ermua, Vizcaya	2
Postal responses					45
					1080

The sample was selected in this manner to allow the influence of large and small surrounding communities to be assessed.

Considering obvious characteristics: occupation, payment level, sex, Basqueness, etc. the data appear to be representative. Thirteen per cent of the respondents to the first survey were female, and 25 per cent individuals describing themselves as 'non Basque'. Thirty two per cent of the sample were below thirty years of age, 37 per cent between thirty and forty, 21 per cent between forty and fifty, and 10 per cent over fifty. (The average age of Mondragon workers was known to be thirty-four). Dates of joining the group spread over the last twenty-two years, with slight clustering over 1967–71. Thirty four per cent of respondents were in low-skilled occupations; semi-skilled and skilled cooperateurs accounted for 27 per cent and 15 per cent respectively, and administrative and managerial staff for 13 per cent and 11 per cent.

Profiles of respondents to the second survey were rather similar, except that there were fewer non-Basques (17 per cent), and more skilled workers. The sample was somewhat younger. Forty eight per cent were below thirty, 35 per cent between thirty and forty, 15 per cent between forty and fifty, and only 7 per cent over fifty.

Profiles of the control are in most respects quite similar. There are somewhat more women (24 per cent) and non-Basques (28 per cent), slightly more unskilled workers, and a more pyramidal wage structure. While age profiles are similar, greater proportions of workers joined the control firms before 1956 and after 1972–6. The former difference reflects Mondragon's rapid growth which reduces the weight of early cohorts; the latter, higher staff turnover in conventional firms.

The most significant difference between sample and control profiles occurs in the proportion of respondents unemployed prior to joining their enterprise. Only 27 per cent of the first Mondragon sample and 42 per cent of the second had not been employed, whereas 55 per cent of the control did not have jobs immediately prior to taking up their current employment. Finally, the selection of the control firms proved to be successful in obtaining respondents familiar with Mondragon. Workers claimed, on the whole, considerable knowledge of the co-operatives; in fact 91 per cent indicated that they had friends or relatives working in the Group.

5   Labor Relations: Cooperative or Conflictual?

Closing the Labor–Capital Gap

This chapter is directed towards understanding the priorities of the Mondragon cooperateurs. Why are their enterprises important to them, if indeed they are? How closely do they appear to identify with their management, and management with them? How far down the occupational and payments scale does ideological solidarity appear to be sustained? The answers to such questions throw some light on the potential contribution of the cooperative organizational form towards X-efficiency, and perhaps, too, on the quality of industrial life in the cooperatives.

The payoff to cooperative organization has long been seen as the elimination of conflict between labor and capital through their internalization in the individual cooperateur. In capitalist enterprises the objectives of different factors of production are unlikely to be identical. Capital (the shareholder) plausibly desires profitability above all. Managers may place a premium on security, pay and status, which they may not consider closely related to profits. Provided workers' jobs are not endangered, a variety of personal objectives may be paramount. Asymmetric information hampers the efficient resolution of disputes through collective bargaining. This divergence of interests and information has been seen to account for widespread X-inefficiency: a situation where the cost curves of enterprises are far above 'optimal' levels, as seen by management, given available technical and organisational possibilities.[1]

Is it not possible to bridge the gap between labor and capital through incentive schemes or integrating workers into the firm along Japanese lines? While some improvement in the alignment of objectives of capital and labor is undoubtedly possible, it seems unlikely that the capital–labor division can be bridged so simply by any of these methods, where there is not already a high degree of social consensus between labor and capital. The total returns to capital may be less than wage costs; equity typically represents only a part of the capital stock. Therefore, unless the fixed wage component is drastically reduced, any profit-related bonuses will be small relative to wage income.

Capitalists will be reluctant to hold equity in enterprises characterised by majority employee shareholding. Such a situation leaves open the possibility that employees, in their capacity as shareholders, may vote themselves wages sufficient to reduce dividends to zero, hence buy out the capitalists at no cost at all. Worker shareholding in capitalist enterprises must therefore remain quite minor. The Western approach to the problem is to reward selected workers – managers – with substantial profit-related incentives and rely on them to enforce the interests of capital throughout the enterprise. Capital–labor tension is transformed into management–labor conflict. The success of such a strategy will depend upon firm-specific factors and the political environment external to the firm. The former include the monitoring and control technology available to managers which, whether more or less effective, probably still permits considerable organisational slack for technical reasons. As described above, the scope for monitoring is undoubtedly circumscribed by external factors where labor possesses a substantial degree of political power. In such cases, the institutional framework of industrial relations will be modified to limit management's ability to manage effectively in the interests of capital.

More obviously, laws may be passed to reduce management's power. Even if legislation does not directly impact on the ability of management to manage, programs cushioning the effects of sanctions will reduce their effectiveness (in a welfare state job loss is less serious) so that a given amount of managerial effort in applying disciplinary measures is less effective. Not so obvious, but sometimes equally important, is the benefit perceived by labor from the *absence* of laws which, although perhaps constraining to management, at least provide clear guidelines for control. In Britain such an attitude has been associated with the tendency for power to shift from national official labor unions to unofficial bodies at plant level.

Workers may benefit from the absence of a formal framework for several reasons. By their nature, legalistic codes at national level are insensitive to the needs of local groups. They also involve elements of compromise which are not acceptable to workers in particular firms in time of a buoyant market, which permits them to take advantage of special circumstances. Workers can press for more in unofficial, sequential, disputes than as an institutionalized component of the political system with broader responsibilities. The value of anarchy to individual workers is shown by the tensions between British Labour Party leadership and its grassroots followers over the period 1960–79.

The timing of the Wagner Act (1935) in the US resulted from the benefit of formal institutionalisation of collective bargaining being greater in adverse labor market conditions. Until recently it has not been possible to sustain labor legislation which curtails union powers (while formalising certain union rights) in Britain. Particularly high unemployment has now eased the passage of the 1982 Employment Act.

The Japanese solution to the problem of industrial conflict treats the symptoms rather than the cause of capital-labor antagonism, softening the mutual opposition of interests with the variety of integrative techniques discussed above. It represents a less complete resolution than the cooperative option, and may be feasible only in specific cultural environments, but avoids the longer-run dynamic instabilities of the cooperative form, discussed in the Mondragon context, below.

Purely technical obstacles to industrial control by management may be minor. But political obstacles can seriously lessen its potential, as has been the case in Italy.[2] It could also be noted that the takeover, the ultimate threat to managerial inefficiency, is powerless to prevent this type of X-inefficiency because new managers are subject to the same economy-wide constraints as old managers. They may, of course, be able to surmount obstacles to efficiency which are internal to the firm. As the general level of industrial efficiency falls short of its potential, so do real incomes and wages relative to those abroad (to preserve the trade balance), which results in lower growth rates of output, real consumption and perhaps investment. The decline of much British manufacturing, in particular the automobile industry over the 1960s and 1970s, would appear to fit this pattern.

All this suggests that the potential for increased productivity due to removing the labor–capital distinction is considerable. How far the potential can be realized is debated, although there is now a body of evidence which suggests that high-trust, cooperative organization may indeed raise productivity.

Productivity and Cooperation
The most extensive comparative study of employee owned firms in the US is that conducted at the Center for Social Research, University of Michigan, by Conte and Tannenbaum (1978). Their investigation analyzed a panel of 98 firms with substantial employee ownership, 68 'beneficially owned' through Employee Stock Ownership Plans (ESOPs) and 30 through direct employee holding of equity. It should be noted that the sample of firms is very different from a sample of Mondragon-like cooperatives. In three-quarters of the ESOP-owned firms, employees actually owned half or more of the total equity, yet in

only 38 per cent of these firms did workers sit on boards of directors. The proportion of companies with workers on boards, 77 per cent, was far higher for directly-owned firms. In such firms it was also more common for employees to vote their stock. Despite these limitations on their power, in 77 per cent of directly employee-owned firms, and in 50 per cent of ESOP firms employees were felt to influence 'important' decisions according to the survey of Conte and Tannenbaum.

Employee ownership appeared to be profitable. Conte and Tannenbaum compared the ratio of profits/sales for the 30 sample firms reporting such information to the average ratios for conventional firms in matching industries. In a number of cases considerably higher pay levels on the employee-owned enterprises reduced reported profitability to below its level as most appropriately measured for comparison. To take this effect into account, profit/sales ratios adjusted for differential pay levels were also computed. Both ratios showed considerable cross-firm variability even within the same industry, which prevented means between the conventional control group and the sample of employee-owned firms from being different at a high level of statistical significance. Unadjusted profitability for employee-owned firms averaged 1.5 times that for control firms while the ratio for adjusted profitability was 1.7. The only structural characteristic significantly associated with higher profitability *within* the employee-owned sample was the share of equity owned by employees, although correlations between a number of characteristics made a conclusive attribution difficult. In the subsample of 30 firms for which the more extensive analysis of profitability could be performed, there was, interestingly, little correlation between the share of equity owned by employees and the percentage of employees owning equity. This peculiar result reflected the highly concentrated pattern of much employee shareholding. Many employees typically owned little or no equity, even in firms owned mostly by employees. This points to a problem in interpreting the study. Many so-called employee owned firms are hard to distinguish from conventional firms with a substantial equity stake by managers.

Conte and Tannenbaum also report a positive attitude to employee ownership on the part of management. Industrial relations were generally felt to be harmonious. Grievances were few, and improved employee cooperation was frequently cited as having contributed to reduced levels of wastage. Management representatives were questioned about the effect of employee ownership on productivity and profit. Their replies were, on average, supportive of employee ownership, to which they were ready to attribute significantly improved attitudes.

Conte and Tannenbaum's results must be interpreted with a degree of caution in inferring causality. Management sufficiently perceptive and progressive to reap the benefits of some employee participation through employee stockholding might also be able to realize greater profitability for other reasons. The sentiments of their study are, however, echoed in the testimony of major corporations before the US Senate Committee on Finance,[3] which credits employee ownership with potential advantages, not only from the viewpoint of the firm but from the perspective of employees. Diluting ownership of capital and raising productivity were also held to be in the national interest.

Other interesting examples are the plywood cooperatives of the Pacific Northwest described by Berman (1967). The earliest of these originated in the early 1920s following the arrival of Scandinavian immigrants with a cooperative tradition. These examples are more relevant to Mondragon because of their rather democractic control systems. Workers have also accumulated equity in individual accounts on similar lines. Some 32 plywood cooperatives are known to have been started since 1930 and by 1978 sixteen were still surviving. Exceptionally for cooperatives, many seem to have been long-lived and successful. Productivity levels 30 per cent above average for the industry were cited as justifying payments levels 25 per cent greater than those paid by competing firms. After investigation by the Internal Revenue Service, concerned that tax advantages be gained by artificially lowering reported profits, this claim was fully accepted.

Other cases, mostly in the United States, in which employee ownership, if not actual cooperative control, appears to have improved productivity through reducing barriers to rationalized resource allocation are documented in Frieden (1979), Oakeshott (1978). Most worker-owned enterprises have arisen out of declining firms, which have been bought by their employees as a desperate expedient to save jobs. In the United States some 70 enterprises converted in this manner in the 1970s. Their performance was reviewed by the Select Committee on Small Business (1979): despite the weakness of most of the firms taken over, in no known case had the employees lost their interest because of closure. The total direct job-preserving effect has been estimated at between 50,000 and 100,000, a figure which local multiplier effects would raise considerably. The picture was less satisfactory in Britain however, for a variety of reasons discussed in Bradley and Gelb (1983).

Unless individuals' priorities can be perfectly aligned (a highly unlikely possibility in any organization where products are produced by individuals acting jointly) a monitoring and control system will be needed to ensure that actions conform to overall objectives. In Western capitalist enterprises control is vertical, from supervisor to supervisee. Cooperatives may improve this vertical monitoring by increasing its acceptability. But additionally, the cooperative form may induce horizontal control, which may be a significant source of economy in formal control costs.

A model of control and incentive structures is presented in the Annex. It is undesirably simplistic, no account being taken of risk or of the dynamic development of the firm. Its main features and conclusions are briefly described here. The defining characteristic of the industrial environment is that information flows are imperfect. Individuals know more about their abilities and the demands of their work than supervisors, who cannot regulate industrial activities without effort. Merely paying an employee in a regular firm a fixed wage provides very little incentive: in such circumstances he will behave optimally from his own perspective without regard for the interests of the firm. Some monitoring system is needed and can only be achieved at a cost. But who supervises the monitors? Somewhere in the firm must be employees who see the structure of their rewards as being linked to firm performance – we term such a limited set the 'managers'. The effectiveness of control is determined by: (a) the response of managers to incentives and (b) the effectiveness of the hierarchical control system. As described above, these factors are likely to be influenced not merely by technological and other factors internal to the firm, but by external constraints; legislation, national union influence and privilege and the attitudes of individual workers which reflect that of society at large.

In contrast to the capitalist firms, a cooperative such as Mondragon distributes profits (the surplus) to its members according to a formula. Capital receives a fixed return and cooperateurs may also receive some component of their income in wage form. Given similar production functions for the cooperative and firm, output varies in a similar manner with comparable changes in the efforts of their employees. There is a similar incentive fund, for wide distribution in the cooperative and narrower disbursement in the firm.

In our model the consequences of wider surplus distribution in the cooperative are two. Firstly, some incentive is given to cooperateurs to align their actions more closely with the interests of their organisations by the direct link between their actions and its profitability. At first sight such a link might seem to be negligible in a firm of conventional size, where surplus is to be shared among several hundred or thousand. The firm however exists because of important complementarities between factors of production within it. These permit the identification of a closer relationship between overall profitability and the efforts of smaller groups. Even so, the direct incentive is likely to be small. This has been recognized as reducing direct incentives to labor in several US worker owned enterprises where exogenous market forces affected bonuses far more than the efforts of individuals.[4]

Nevertheless the sum of small direct incentives over the workforce may result in improved vertical control. Collective appreciation by cooperateurs of their management as their own delegated authority could inhibit the development of attitudes, informal agreements and collective understandings which serve to frustrate attempts at vertical control. This is only likely to occur in the event that high-trust relations between managerial and non-managerial grades of cooperateur can be maintained. In this case, labor (or the labor component) agrees to align its priorities more closely with those of capital (or the capital component commonly identified with the firm). Such a situation may contribute to cooperative efficiency but is unlikely to completely satisfy more ideological supporters of cooperativism, because the function of employee ownership is only to permit conventional operations to proceed more smoothly – the cooperative becomes an assembly of self-exploiting workers.

An appreciation of the complementarities between cooperateurs is likely to lead to another, indirect, incentive operating through monitoring and encouragement between them. This horizontal monitoring, though it may be limited for any single individual, can be significant in aggregate because all are involved. Indeed, it can be shown (see Annex) that, under fairly general assumptions, broader distribution of a given incentive pool results in greater aggregate work effort if there are increasing marginal disutilities to monitoring. It may also induce greater aggregate monitoring effort. Factors favouring a narrow distribution of incentives include (a) economies of scale in monitoring, (b) social or technological factors rendering horizontal control ineffectual, and (c) differences between individuals in their intrinsic preferences for monitoring. Cooperateurs may therefore tend to create for themselves a more 'disciplined' environment, although it is not clear that they themselves will perceive it as being more disciplined. The different nature of the incentive system induces members to align their priorities with those of the firm without compulsion.

This may substitute for other methods of securing greater alignment of individual and collective goals. For example, it may not be necessary to introduce job-enrichment experiments (such as that at Volvo–Kalma) in cooperatives because there is less need to combat the buildup of antagonistic tendencies among the workforce.

How effective is such horizontal control? The critical factors seem to be two. Firstly, to what extent *can* workers at different levels monitor and judge the work performance of others? Secondly, *do* the norms of society favour or discourage positive reinforcement between workers at similar levels?

Production technology plays a large role in circumscribing monitoring possibilities. Technological determinists view physical plant as dictating work behaviour and as predetermined at a particular moment in a given social system.[5] An alternative view would admit a spectrum of technological variation and allow a range of behaviour – perhaps associated with plant layout – in a given technology. But considerable scope for lateral control appears to exist regardless of technological constraints. Only some 2 per cent of all Americans employed in manufacturing are estimated to work in assembly line-like conditions despite the prominence of this kind of work in traditional industrial relations emphasizing the role of collective bargaining. Lower occupations may be less constrained, direct supervisory possibilities of many high-level staff are restricted. Surveys conducted in several British and American companies by one of the authors leave no doubt that a large proportion of the typical workforce sees substantial opportunities for informal monitoring of fellow workers.

In practice the second constraint on positive reinforcement, that of deviant industrial norms, should be less in cooperative society. Under favorable market conditions it should also be less in Japanese-style industry because of the promise of lifetime employment and payment by age. It remains to be seen how well it survives the recent tendency for meritocratic promotion to be superimposed on the lifetime system in Japan, and enforced early retirement of workers because of an adverse economic climate. In traditional Western firms there may be large barriers to positive reinforcement because the payoff to greater efficiency does not accrue immediately and directly to the workers involved. The output responses of a given firm to reductions in its cost levels through innovation may be slow, because of the need to broaden product lines, break into new markets and adapt quality to compete with other producers. Therefore in the short-medium term, increased labor efficiency is reflected in a reduced workforce and lower trust.[6] In the last resort the possibility of horizontal monitoring and whether it actually takes place are empirical questions.

Identifying with the Firm in Mondragon

Cooperatives might induce fundamental changes in economic man, or they might not. Underlying the present discussion is the same self-centered individualistic human model common to conventional economic theory. Perhaps cooperatives can lead to a greater weighting of the welfare of others in individual preferences, hence internalize some of the externalities between members, but there is no obvious way of testing this proposition. Some internalization is quite likely at Mondragon, given the close identification of many cooperateurs with their communities and the criteria for selection described above. It is also likely that distinctive individuals, those placing high priority on cooperativism, will be attracted to cooperatively run enterprises, so that selection biases will affect estimates of causality from economic organization to individual behaviour. Whatever the possibilities for changing human nature, survey results below suggest that traditional economic motives still prevail in the cooperatives.

Objective measures of preference-intensity cannot, of course, be constructed. Respondents were asked to rank factors concerning their enterprise in order of importance as perceived by themselves. Two sets of factors were distinguished. Extrinsic factors – level of payments and job security – relate primarily to economic reward, while instrinsic factors – the 'Basqueness' of the enterprise and its cooperative nature *per se* cover other aspects. A similar choice was presented to the control except that good working conditions replaced cooperative nature as a proxy for intrinsic value. Table 5.1 indicates rankings over these alternatives as seen by respondents for their own firms, and as seen by the control for Mondragon.

Table 5.1   Perceived importance of enterprise characteristics*

	Ranking of Cooperatives by Cooperateurs			
	1	*2*	*3*	*4*
Cooperative	619	228	93	37
Job security	324	411	268	29
Basqueness	81	244	284	199
Payments	31	102	292	484
	Ranking of Control Firms by their Workers			
	1	*2*	*3*	*4*
Working conditions	65	97	45	21
Job security	119	58	36	20
Basqueness	65	39	41	86
Payments	33	45	69	66
	Ranking of Cooperatives by Control Workers			
	1	*2*	*3*	*4*
Cooperative	118	69	27	15
Job security	98	72	37	21
Basqueness	26	34	44	117
Payments	42	50	90	43

* Column and row totals are not equal because of the inclusion of partial rankings offered by some respondents. No conclusions are altered by their deletion.

The overwhelming priority on cooperativism runs through all levels of the Mondragon workforce across all characteristics of respondents. This suggests that the emphasis placed officially on cooperativism is mirrored in the attitude of the workforce. Although Mondragon workers undoubtedly have far greater job security than conventional workers, this ranks a clear second. It ranks as a prime concern of the control where working environment is second. Differences in first rankings between subject and control groups are significant at the 1 percent level on a Chi-square test. Payments and Basqueness are of generally lower priority, and orderings between these two alternatives reverse between Basques and non-Basques. The control group also singled out worker involvement and job security as the most distinctive features of the cooperatives relative to their own firm.

A rough guide to the intensity with which various options are perceived as important by the members as a whole is the extent to which there is consensus on the ordering. High consensus indicates that the enterprise is not 'factionalized' into groups with very different views. Table 5.1 indicates a rather clear priority on cooperative nature and job security over Basqueness and pay. Only 11 per cent of cooperateurs ranked either of the latter as the most important feature of the cooperatives. On the control however, the various attributes of their own enterprise received considerably more uniform emphasis, with 35 per cent emphasizing the least two important features.

To assess differences in cooperative and firm working conditions subject and control groups were asked comparable questions focusing on environmental receptivity. Did they sometimes feel prevented from voicing opinions and grievances? Was a gulf perceived between management and workers? Was a role seen for trade unions within their enterprise? A role for trade unions is taken as an indicator of a perceived conflict of interests between capital and labor. Results are shown in Tables 5.2, 5.3 and 5.4. Table 5.2 suggests a somewhat more favourable environment in the cooperatives than in the control. However, over 40 per cent of cooperateurs indicated that sometimes they felt inhibited from expressing opinions. Dissatisfaction and conflict do indeed exist in the cooperatives. Women and non-Basques, for example, are more prone to experience representational difficulties. As described below, there appears also to be a 'generation gap' in Mondragon, although whether this relates to the vintage of cooperateurs or simply to age is not clear. The circumstances under which individuals joined the Group, in particular whether they were previously employed, also appear to affect responses.

Mondragon managers and specialists, as well as workers, sometimes experience frustrations with work in the Group, and also feel the pull of

Table 5.2   Perceived difficulty of representation

	Cooperatives	%	Firms	%
Sometimes inhibited from expressing opinions, etc.	415	41	117	55
Not inhibited	589	59	95	45
Total	1,004	100	212	100

Chi-square$_1$ = 43.7: significant at 0.005.

Table 5.3   Perceived division between management and workers

	Cooperatives	%	Firms	%
Large division	209	21	164	62
Small division	583	59	65	25
No division	200	20	36	13
Total	992	100	265	100

Chi-square$_2$ = 328.2: significant at 0.005.

Table 5.4   Support for large trade-union role in enterprise

	Cooperatives	%	Firms	%
Yes	242	25	225	86
No	729	75	36	14
Total	971	100	261	100

Chi-square$_1$ = 328.2: significant at 0.005.

higher outside pay levels to a greater extent. Management of individual cooperatives is normally drawn from the group proposing the establishment of the new enterprise to the Caja. Appointment is usually for a period of about four years, although frequently the Caja is forced to step in and change management. Because of low pay and a shortage of local skills, attempts to restrict the recruitment of managers to the local community often are unsuccessful. There is however only a small perceived division between workers and management in the cooperatives, in contrast to the situation on the control firms. This difference is not too surprising since Mondragon managers often earn less than half the salary of managers in comparable firms, and also have far less security of tenure in the management positions. It is not unusual for a deposed Mondragon manager to move to another cooperative in a non-managerial capacity. Although the cooperatives have found difficulty in attracting and holding managers and technical specialists they have succeeded in combining industry and an almost classless society.[7] However, the drive towards increasing the range of pay differentials from 1:3 towards 1:4.5 came largely from younger, dissatisfied managers and specialists. The purity of cooperative ideals is thus under stress from economic man and the pull of the labor market.

Trade union activity poses far less of a direct threat to solidarity. The role of unions in workers cooperatives has been widely debated in a number of countries. The official trade-union view of worker-owned enterprises has not been favourable, because of a perception that they undermine the traditional process of collective bargaining.[8] Unions have also opposed cooperatives on grounds of increased risk to worker-shareholders. Local and national union priorities diverge, however, when closing capitalist firms are taken over by workers to preserve jobs and local groups have sometimes spearheaded takeovers.

Proponents of cooperatives are usually also proponents of labor. They have therefore often found themselves in the position of having to reconcile support for employee ownership with advocacy of a continuing role for unions. This is only possible by recognizing a change in the union function, away from national or industry-wide representation and collective bargaining and towards the role of a 'loyal opposition' internal and specific to the firm.[9] This approaches the company unionism so characteristic of Japanese corporations, and represents a definite weakening in the regulatory powers of unions.

It is not at all clear what role unions can play on cooperatives, especially those with democratic ownership and control systems. The vast majority of Mondragon cooperateurs see no role for trade unions in their enterprises, in contrast to the control group sample. Part of the support for unions derives from their link with Basque nationalism, a factor which would tend to encourage a positive view in the intensely nationalistic cooperatives. Cooperative management has barred industrial action in sympathy from groups outside the cooperative. However, there is more support for unions among young cooperateurs of recent vintage.

Most ominously for trade unions, despite their strong support for an enhanced union role in their own enterprises, 52 per cent of control group workers expressing a preference between cooperative structure and trade unionism as vehicles for advancement of labor chose the former. Presented with a viable alternative, labor may not choose the confrontational option. It is an interesting question whether the spread of Japanese-style management techniques in a depressed labor market will similarly undermine traditional collective bargaining in the United States and Britain through demonstration effects.

Can we be sure that concepts such as 'worker-management distance' are perceived similarly by the subject and control groups? A partial check was attempted by asking the control to assess this separation on the cooperatives relative to that in their own firms. Fifty-seven per cent considered the Mondragon division to be far smaller while only 4 per cent considered it to be greater. This perception accords well with Table 5.3. Differences in manager–worker identification cannot easily be traced to third, 'social' variables. For example, while most cooperateurs have friends and relatives working in their enterprises (which may allow personal relationships to span hierarchy) so do most members of the control.

Perceptions of job control and of participation also support the hypothesis that Mondragon offers a more favourable work environment. Seventy seven per cent of cooperateurs consider that the cooperative nature of their enterprise allows them a greater measure of job control than they would have in a conventional firm. Participation perceptions are shown in Table 5.5.

Table 5.5   Perceived degree of participation in important decisions

	Cooperatives	%	Firms	%
Direct participation	128	13	10	4
Indirect participation*	198	20	9	3
Not very extensive participation	272	27	38	14
No participation	395	30	212	80
Total	993	100	269	100

Chi-square$_3$ = 134.0: significant at 0.005.
* Participation through representatives rather than directly.

This difference in perceptions may be partly subjective rather than due merely to objective differences. It cannot be ascribed to differing occupational proportions in sample and control. Indeed, one of the more intriguing features of the responses is that even managerial grades in the control respond less positively than do many lower-grade cooperateurs. But in the final analysis, which is more important: that individuals participate or that they feel that they do? We leave this question open. In sum, while not conforming to an ideal model of equal participation, the perceived cooperative environments perform far better than those of the control.

Cooperatives may raise efficiency if, through promoting high-trust relationships between capital, management and labor, they prevent the emergence of attitudes inhibiting vertical control. Capital–labor contradiction cannot directly be assessed since cooperateurs are equity and labor combined, yet in its role as managerial and financial overseer of Mondragon the Caja Laboral Popular plays one part of the capitalist role, while as development bank and mobilizer of private capitalist savings it plays another part. Despite the ultimate obligation to its depositors, out of 973 responses, 82 per cent of cooperateurs considered the Caja really to support the interests of Mondragon workers.

How this solidarity weathers the adverse economic conditions at the start of the 1980s remains to be seen. In 1979 managers of the industrial plants were receptive to the oversight of the Caja and trusted it to support their enterprises through difficulty. Surveys of management conducted in 1982 suggest a souring of relations. Recession had sharpened the divergence between the Caja's roles of saving bank and development agency for the cooperative group. [10]

With whom do cooperateurs identify? In Table 5.6 groups are ranked according to the degree to which their actions were felt to most closely further the interests of cooperateurs. Overall, cooperative managers followed by cooperative workers are felt to best represent the sample's interest. Basque and Spanish workers come a poor third and fourth, respectively. Worker-manager trust in Mondragon is revealed again in the second part of the Table where cooperative managers tend to rank cooperative workers in first place. Similarly, cooperative workers rank their managers in first place. This is an especially impressive result given the tight discipline of the cooperatives.

Table 5.6   Ranking of groups according to representation of interests

	Ranking by							
	Cooperateurs Overall				*Cooperative Managers*			
	1	*2*	*3*	*4*	*1*	*2*	*3*	*4*
Cooperative manager	201	97	63	38	16	16	12	2
Cooperative workers	152	206	63	38	24	19	2	2
Basque workers generally	70	76	107	46	7	10	23	3
Spanish workers generally	22	23	60	249	2	3	4	33

High trust in management by rank and file cooperateurs does not imply an absence of criticism. Cooperateurs are highly critical of their management who consequently have unusually short tenure, as discussed in the following chapter.

6 Consensus, Reinforcement and Accountability

Hierarchical and Lateral Accountability

To maintain a favourable industrial environment within any firm involves both positive reinforcement of employee initiative and negative sanctions against seriously counterproductive behaviour. How far these are possible depends on both the response of individual workers and that of their representative organizations such as trade unions and worker councils. These may create a climate supportive of management or one designed to frustrate at every turn.

The scientifically-managed firm serves to emphasize the role of negative sanctions relative to the Japanese model. Motivational workplace problems are seen as inevitable, to be eliminated by more sophisticated monitoring systems rather than by taking workers into the confidence of their firms. This breaks down when society bars or hinders the use of scientific management techniques or, through laws or social security, renders sanctions ineffective. An emphasis on group responsibility and on integrating workers with their organizations leads Japanese-style firms to reinforce the positive aspects of worker–management relations, but capital and labor still have distinct interests which may resurface when market conditions deteriorate. It may also be harder to take workers into the confidence of the firm if it lacks a degree of monopoly power to act as a cushion against the risks of failure.

The absence of a theoretical divide between capital and labor on Mondragon cooperatives has been shown to be reflected in an unusually cohesive workforce, with few dissenting loyalties despite imperfections in the working environment. Is this reflected in peer–group pressures to align individual actions towards collective goals?

A distinction must be drawn between formal and informal supervision. Informal supervision describes the activities of individual workers which involve monitoring and encouraging their fellows. A rough guide to the potential for such monitoring is to assess how many workers each individual considers himself able to monitor in the course of work, and to subtract formal supervisory duties from this. Then it is necessary to judge how far this potential is realized, and why.

Formal supervisory responsibilities for cooperative and control groups are shown in Table 6.1. The profiles are virtually identical, largely because the organization of work in Mondragon is conventional. This suggests that any peer group monitoring is used to supplement, rather than to replace, formal control.

Table 6.1   Formal supervision

Workers formally supervised	Cooperatives	%	Firms	%
None	641	69	169	67
1–5	120	13	30	12
6–10	56	6	18	7
11–20	28	3	5	2
Over 20	88	9	31	12
Total	993	100	253	100

Chi-square$_4$ = 2.9: not significant at 0.500.

If technology severely limited the potential for horizontal control, there would be little point in extending incentives to encourage it. To establish the potential for such 'un-official' control, respondents were asked to estimate the number of workers on their enterprises that they felt able to observe and encourage in their duties. Results are shown in Table 6.2. Again there is no large difference between the profiles.

Table 6.2   Monitoring possibilities

Number able to be observed	Cooperatives	%	Firms	%
None	316	35	100	42
1–5	237	26	54	23
6–10	119	13	28	12
11–20	89	10	17	7
Over 20	139	15	39	17
Total	900	100	238	100

Chi-square$_3$ = 5.3: not significant at 0.250.

The difference between Tables 6.1 and 6.2 understates the potential for informal supervision since formal supervisory duties exceed, in many cases, the number respondents felt able to monitor. This is true on both the cooperatives and control. On the cooperatives the volume of potential informal supervision (as crudely measured by the integral over respondents of the excess of their potential over their formal supervision estimates) equals that of formal supervision. Slightly smaller, but still very substantial possibilities for informal supervision appear to exist on the control.

Informal supervision may not materialize if the general consensus denies the importance of work effort in furthering the goals of the enterprise. This is the case neither in the cooperative nor in the control although the latter group is slightly more ready to ascribe success to other factors: see Table 6.3. Responses to this question do not depend sensitively upon occupation.

Table 6.3   Belief in dependence of enterprise success upon special effort of workforce

	Cooperatives	%	Firms	%
Yes	844	84	198	76
No	158	16	63	24
Total	1,002	100	261	100

Chi-square$_1$ = 10.1: significant at 0.005.

Workers therefore have the opportunity to encourage and monitor each other well in excess of their formal responsibilities, and recognize the role of good performance in the success of their enterprise. These are in fact typical of responses to surveys of firms in industrial countries. However, the response of cooperateurs to the question of whether informal encouragement is *actually* given differs quite substantially from that of control workers. See Table 6.4.

Cooperatives do indeed appear able to induce horizontal reinforcement to strengthen and complement traditional vertical control. Vertical control is itself plausibly rendered more effective by the strengthening of vertical high-trust relationships as shown in Table 5.6. Finally, the dependence of the Mondragon work ethic upon the interaction of two factors: (a) the belief that success depends upon the efforts of the workforce, and (b) the shareholding of cooperateurs in their enterprises, is illustrated in Table 6.5.

Table 6.4   Informal control

Workers encourage each other	Cooperatives	%	Firms	%
A great deal	160	38	53	21
A little	163	38	68	27
Not at all (only supervisors)	99	23	133	52
Total	422[1]	100	254	100

Chi-square$_2$ = 59.7: significant at 0.005.

Table 6.5   The cooperative work ethic

Investments as factor in belief that cooperateurs should work well	Belief in importance of special effort in success				
	Yes	%	No	%	Total
Extremely strong	374	80	43	50	417
Weak	92	20	43	50	135
Total	466	100	86	100	552

Chi-square$_1$ = 36.0: significant at 0.005.

More efficient work need not imply longer or harder hours. Theoretically there is no reason why preference for leisure should not dominate the choices of workers as the income received per hour rises. Any efficiency gains achieved on the cooperatives seem not to be appropriated by workers in the form of leisure. This is noteworthy because they cannot benefit much in terms of *current* income from harder work if wage solidarity is maintained with surrounding firms. Only 2 per cent of cooperateurs considered themselves to be working less hard on their enterprises than they would on a conventional firm while over half considered that they worked significantly harder. Whether cooperateurs *actually* work harder is, of course, another matter, although control perceptions of cooperative discipline (see below) suggest that they do. So do cooperative managers who view the intensity of work in Spanish industry as a 'disaster' and easily surpassed. They are less sanguine over competing with Japanese and other European industry. However, in assessing the impact of cooperative structure on efficiency, the subjective view is at least as important as the objective, since it indicates the direction in which group pressure is felt to act. Short of a rigorous work-study exercise we see no way of assessing objectively work intensity differences.

Under Mondragon rules, cooperateurs accumulate capital at a fairly uniform rate because pay scales, on which surplus distributions are based, are compressed. Vintage of cooperateur, capital holdings and age are therefore correlated. The importance of an individual's capital holding as a motivating factor would be expected to rise with the size of account, therefore with the length of association of the individual with Mondragon. Data support this hypothesis: cooperateurs of earlier vintage are more likely to stress the importance of their investments as motivating their belief that fellow cooperateurs should work productively; see Table 6.6.

Table 6.6   Vintage and the effect of investment

Year of joining cooperatives	Investment as factor in belief that cooperateurs should work well				
	Strong	*%*	*Weak*	*%*	*Total*
Before 1961	90	12	13	6	103
1962–71	420	56	126	53	546
After 1972	245	32	98	41	343
	755	100	237	100	992

Chi-square$_2$ = 11.5: significant at 0.005.

This can also reflect a competing hypothesis – that attitudes to the cooperative differ with age. The experience of Mondragon parallels that of industrial society at large, in that younger workers have aspirations and horizons broader than those of the earlier generation. This hypothesis has been investigated by Kornhauser (1965) who finds that younger workers are more radical and adopt a more critical attitude to existing arrangements. That age rather than generational or other social factors is important is also suggested by Bradley (1983). The difference may be more acute in the Basque provinces because of the restricted political environment which prevailed before the death of Franco. This is compounded by the tendency of younger workers to have been recruited in periods of higher unemployment, which results in a larger proportion of new entrants being attracted to the cooperative group because of a need for jobs. Data are insufficient to separate out the age and vintage effects convincingly.

How do the above factors combine to influence the disciplinary environment of a cooperative relative to that of a firm? This is far from being a simple question, not only because of the lack of any objective measure of discipline, but because two offsetting tendencies induced by cooperativism influence subjective assessments of the nature and rigor of control.

On the one hand both formal and informal controls are likely to be stronger on a cooperative. Formal control is easier because of vertical trust; horizontal control is encouraged by joint shareholding. However, the same forces encouraging control are responsible for aligning individual priorities more closely with that of their enterprise. By reducing the need for control, this will also reduce individual perceptions of being subject to control. From the outside, the cooperatives should appear as well disciplined. A high degree of acquiescence to discipline and, therefore, a somewhat less disciplined *impression* should prevail inside. This qualitative difference between insider and outsider views of discipline and in particular the role of self-discipline, was suggested in a number of interviews as an important element of the Mondragon employment relations environment:

> From the outside Mondragon is seen a a strict place of discipline. . . .
> However, our members are encouraged to think that they are not just workers but managers. As a manager a person has to realize just how far a worker's demands are feasible. There is no self-management without self-discipline.[2]

Survey data provide some support for these hypotheses, as shown in Table 6.7. While perceptions of the cooperatives as disciplined rather than undisciplined enterprises prevail both in the survey and in interviews, the external view is significantly more inclined towards tighter discipline. This difference is plausibly associated with the alignment of individual and enterprise goals in the cooperatives. Only 4 per cent of cooperateurs indicated disagreement with the way in which discipline was implemented. Of the other 96 per cent, almost half endorsed discipline as 'strict' while the remainder considered it moderate.

Table 6.7   Discipline of cooperatives relative to firms

View of cooperatives relative to firms	*Cooperatives*	%	*Firms*	%
More disciplined	392	39	129	49
Similar	383	39	128	48
Less disciplined	222	22	8	3
Total	997	100	265	100

Chi-square$_2$ = 52.1: significant at 0.005.

To obtain objective indications of discipline is indeed difficult. However, one verification of the combined effects of self and conventional discipline on the cooperatives is provided by the observation that absences due to 'illness' have been, on average, about half those on comparable local firms.[3] The results of our survey suggest that Mondragon's cooperative nature permits the maintenance of a disciplined environment without overtly constraining individual behaviour.

Management on the Cooperatives

An unusual feature of Mondragon is the extent to which discipline and accountability run two ways, both up and down the vertical hierarchy. Cooperateurs are very critical of management. The result is high enforced mobility of managers, unlike the situation in local conventional firms:

> On the cooperatives we have no pity. When a manager is not performing well the cooperateurs soon get rid of him. Cooperateurs believe that management *must* resolve problems and if they don't, they're changed. In a year often 12 cases [out of some 80 cooperatives] occur where managers are dismissed. Managers are aware that they must succeed in order to maintain their jobs. Managers have often to justify their policies before the Junta Rectora and the collective.[4]

Worker shareholders are likely to exert a more effective influence on their management than conventional corporate shareholders for two reasons. Firstly, they are less dispersed and do not vote by proxy as directed by the Board. Secondly, because they are inside the firm, they have better access to information than most shareholders, and are perhaps more aware of management errors. Surveys of conventional firms in the US and Britain conducted by one of the authors over the last three years show that even contented workers in firms with harmonious relations are highly critical of managerial competence.

Too much accountability of management may backfire in that it may be blamed for exogenous factors which reduce profitability. Unfair criticism of managers was cited as a particular problem at Mondragon because of the difficulty of recruiting experienced managers from outside. To compensate, Mondragon is therefore forced to 'take risks by employing young people who haven't reached their ceiling and who find in the cooperative status, responsibility and creativity'. The development of managerial and specialist talent makes such experienced Mondragon personnel particularly attractive to outside firms. They are held in the cooperatives through a variety of social, moral and ideological ties. But frustration with performing their tasks must be kept within reasonable bounds and growth must offer exciting opportunities. There is thus a positive feedback from growth to cooperative solidarity through retaining talent within the narrow differential range.

Following a period during which restrictive labor practices have been held responsible for slowing productivity growth in the industrialized economies, attention has been shifting to the role of management in poor performance. With the traditional accountability of management in Western firms, shareholder *putsches* and takeover raids determine the extent to which management can satisfice, work in the interests of other groups or simply perform poorly.[5] Accountability to workers is violently resisted by managers in conventional firms as eroding their prerogatives, which are supported by principles of scientific management. On the other hand, the spread of such innovations as quality circles suggests that labor is eager to contribute detailed knowledge of production processes to raise efficiency. This threatens middle management in particular, who are not supposed to be accountable to subordinates. Mondragon confirms that accountability to workers is likely to be rather rigorous. It may do well with the managerial talent it has, but this is restricted because lower pay and tight accountability defines a smaller pool from which managers can be recruited.

7 Industrial Democracy and Small Communities

Ethnicity, Community and the Cooperative Option

The main ways in which solidarity benefits the cooperatives therefore appear to be rather as expected from a simple theoretical analysis of the benefits of internalizing the capital–labor division within individual cooperateurs. Given the improved climate of labor relations why are cooperatives so few? Are there environments more conducive to cooperative-type organizations: for example, are they more appropriate for regional development than for urban regeneration? Can the gains be obtained without experiencing some of the evident drawbacks which must prevent cooperatives from assuming a dominant role in capitalist countries?

Any bond which encourages members of a firm to identify with each other across functional specializations and hierarchy is likely to encourage cooperative behavior. Ethnicity is one obvious bond. The homogeneity and cultural isolation of Japanese society are often seen as factors contributing to the success of the paternalism–lifetime–commitment model. The Z firms appear more homogeneous than their counterpart A firms. The 'Basqueness' of Mondragon has been held to be of great importance to its success and consequently a barrier to its replication.[1] Ethnicity is occasionally seen as a positive feature for Mondragon's replicability. For example, the appeal of the model has been enhanced in South Wales because of two perceived similarities, physical isolation and a distinctive culture.[2]

Both cultural and political factors specific to the Basque region have been highlighted by other studies as providing a foundation receptive to ideas of self-management. The Basque propensity to save is believed to be high relative to that of other working people. Basques see themselves as serious-minded and hardworking relative to their Castilian neighbours. High-trust relations between workers are said to have been generated over the decades through working men's drinking clubs. The traditional role of such clubs as small-scale credit unions has also facilitated collective fund raising. On the political side, the Spanish central government has sought since Franco to unify the country. Spanish nationalism has manifested itself in continuing repression of Basque cultural activity and expression:

> In the Basque country . . . one will be reminded of the suppression of regional cultures by the Franco regime and its servants . . . a detachment of the Civil Guard, led by a lieutenant, burst into the cinema of the Basque town of Mondragon to interrupt a pre-Christmas festival of Basque songs and music . . . The guards ordered the packed audience to leave and, after one minute, began firing rubber bullets and smoke grenades . . . Last year, after a shoot-out near Mondragon between Civil Guards and ETA terrorists, many of the town's citizens applauded the ETA men. A few weeks ago 500 people held pro-ETA demonstrations in the town centre. (*The Economist*, November 3, 1979)

A common external threat has traditionally been the strongest incentive for unity. Repression may have provided a binding force and strengthened consensus among the Basque people. In the absence of such unusual circumstances it may be harder to create and sustain successful cooperatives.

Despite these binding forces, the ethnic dimension is not so simple. 'Basqueness' is subjective, rather than objective. Historically, the Basque country has always drawn and assimilated immigrants, mainly from the South of Spain. Ethnic origin is not an overriding factor on the cooperatives. The real distinction is between those who have integrated themselves with their local community and those who have not. This is considered an important selection criterion, and more important than the degree of Basque ethnicity.

Nevertheless, Mondragon does emphasize 'Basqueness' in selection. At the beginning it was perhaps more open than it has since become, since few locals had the financial ability to contribute to cooperative funds and to take the risk which joining the cooperative entailed. In early years, local workers stood to lose not only their financial stakes, but the prospects of another job in the area because conventional employers opposed the formation of the cooperative. But particularly when labor markets slackened in the late 1960s, the pressure to employ local Basques, especially those related to existing cooperateurs, intensified. Today, even managers acknowledging the cooperatives' indebtness to the efforts of 'foreign' members would unhesitatingly give preference to local Basque recruits. A second characteristic of the Mondragon environment is its physical isolation, which brings closer together the firm and the community. Mondragon in fact does emphasize the degree of integration into local communities by preferentially hiring children of cooperateurs although this is not a formal criterion. The group strengthens its community links by developing social and welfare services.

When their survival is threatened communities can exert strong pressures for cooperative solutions, but only when the individuals involved are part of the community.[3] The success of the Jamestown Labor–Management committee in attracting industry to a declining area is one notable example of this potential.[4] There is a general tendency for employee-owned firms to exist in small towns and rural environments. About three-quarters of the cases of worker buyouts cited in Bradley and Gelb (1983) had such dependent communities as did the plywood cooperatives. Most Z-firms also started in small towns. The role of the community in attempts to establish worker-owned firms in the US has been considerable, as described by Zwerdling (1978). Casual evidence therefore suggests that the potential of cooperatives is greatest when applied to regional development. The anonymity of a larger urban environment and the closeness of alternative reference groups pose an obstacle to a unitary model of industrial organization.

There is a more specific reason why cooperatives are likely to flourish in isolated areas. The tradeoff between solidarity, efficiency and autonomy from outside investors is less acute because of the adverse effect of labor mobility on the accumulation of equity when this is held in individual accounts as in Mondragon. The total capital stock of an enterprise may be broken down into loan capital and equity or own resources where the latter accepts the residual return. Equity must remain in the hands of cooperateurs for them to be capable of taking autonomous decisions.[5] Even with good access to loan capital gearing limits restrict available assets/man to a set multiple of equity/man. Setting aside the difficulty of raising sufficient equity to start up, the problem in the long run is to maintain equity levels which allow accommodation to technical change and sustain growth.

Difficulties of cooperatives in the US and Britain have been ascribed partly to the reluctance of bankers to lend to them: see, for example, Thornley (1981) and Rothschild-Whitt (1979). Mondragon, through the establishments of the Caja Laboral Popular has relaxed this total capital constraint, but a potential equity constraint remains. Debt/equity ratios have risen slightly in Mondragon, but are still conservative.

Strong community ties lower labor mobility and reduce the desire of cooperateurs to withdraw capital while working for the enterprise. Regionalized populations of low mobility are plausibly less inclined to remit capital to other geographical areas. Withdrawals by existing cooperateurs may be limited by regulation but only if consensus on the desirability of limitations is maintained. Individual equity shares must also be withdrawn by departing cooperateurs if control is to be maintained within the enterprise. Assuming that new cooperateurs are unable or unwilling to immediately replace equity withdrawn by retiring members, equity/man ratios decline because the cooperative must seek loans on behalf of its new members.

To some extent this problem can be overcome by communally-owned equity. Some managers see the augmentation of the common reserve as a necessary development at Mondragon to preserve the cooperatives from decapitalization by retiring workers. Communally-owned capital raises the problems of accumulation, risk and incentive. It reduces incentives to reinvestment of cooperative surplus. In the short term accumulation may be protected by rules but these depend in the longer-run on their acceptability. Even if reinvestment rules are applied, communal ownership breaks the link between individual con-tribution and reward, unless current income bears the burden of all fluctuations in earnings (rather like the taxi driver who pays a fixed rent for his cab). This shifts risk onto the current incomes of the workforce to an undesirable, and probably unacceptable, extent. The disad-vantages of communal ownership probably outweigh the benefits.

In Mondragon, equity is accumulated by members in the course of their employment through retentions of corporate surplus in individual accounts. Let L_i be the number of cooperative workers who joined i years ago and X_i be the average equity/man accumulated by a cooperateur in cohort i. Unless the cooperative shrinks, $L_{i+1} < L_i$ but $X_{i+1} > X_i$. The average equity/man, E, is given by:

$$E = \sum_i X_i L_i / \sum_i L_i.$$

The higher is the proportion of long-serving cooperateurs, the higher will be E. Mobile labor and retirement therefore both constrain equity and capital accumulation, and place an upper bound on the capital intensity of cooperatives. Unless labor can easily be retrained or switched without costs to the organization, technical and product change poses a dilemma for cooperatives in their attitude to older members. They have too much capital invested to be be encouraged to leave prematurely, but maintaining them as members may be costly in terms of labor productivity.

The Local Community and Mondragon

Basque nationalism is indeed strong in Mondragon. In the first demo-cratic elections after Franco's death 48 per cent of our respondents voted for Basque extreme left-wing parties and another 40 per cent for Basque nationalists. Within the cooperatives, the official language is Basque (although members can speak Castilian) and there is some pressure on non-Basque speakers to learn the language. However, Basqueness is not seen as an overridingly significant feature of Mondragon either by cooperateurs or by workers in other local firms. This was shown in Table 5.1, where rankings over four characteristics were quite similar between the cooperateurs and control. The most distinctive features were considered to be the Group's cooperative nature and security of employment. Far behind came the ethnic nature of the cooperatives and their level of payments.

While from outside of the Basque provinces the ethnic dimension is accredited strong causal significance, from inside, against the backdrop of general Basqueness this characteristic is far less important. Although 80 per cent of cooperateurs describe themselves as Basque, so do 72 per cent of the control. The gulf between Mondragon and Basque workers as perceived by cooperateurs appears in some sense to be sharper than that perceived between Basque and Spanish workers: see Table 5.2. There is no evidence that ethnic Basqueness blunts the capital/labor divide on the conventional Basque control.

The common Basque heritage probably assists Mondragon as it minimizes serious cultural fragmentation within the enterprise, but the Basque country itself is not homogenous:

> . . . Basqueness counts, but more important is whether prospective members are inhabitants of the local community in which the cooperative is situated. The Basque country . . . is also municipally autonomous. People from Mondragon feel very different from those of Vergura or Onate which is only 8 kms. away. So, what is important is that members are drawn from a specific community and not just the Basque country. One of the factors which has contributed to the success of Mondragon is a definite feeling of community. Because of the community factor we refer to the cooperatives as the *Mondragon experience*: the experience was born in Mondragon, supported locally and supported by people from the local community. The Mondragon experience is very much identified with and integrated with the local community.[6]

The uniqueness of Mondragon's organization suggests that its members should have a strong attachment to the cooperatives and be less eager to move in response to pay differentials than workers on conventional firms. This is borne out by survey results. Tables 7.1 and 7.2 suggest that few cooperateurs would transfer to local firms even with large pay incentives (they were also asked to assume that complete capital withdrawal was possible). They are slightly more ready to consider transferring to a hypothetical 'Spanish' cooperative but even this is not an attractive option.

This result is not inconsistent with the low priority placed on 'Basqueness' in Table 5.1. Against a generally Basque backdrop, the strongly Basque nature of the cooperatives is far less marked. The well-known strength of Basque nationalism actually provides, through Table 7.2, an impressive verification of the strength of 'cooperativism' as a perceived feature of the Mondragon group.

Integration into a tight, close-knit community was argued above to be a potentially important factor in preserving the equity of a cooperative. Mondragon provides strong support for this hypothesis, if we interpret respondents claiming to be non-Basque to be those not integrated into their communities: see Table 7.3. It is clear that the close balance between those desiring to withdraw capital and those content with the *status quo* is maintained only by the proportion of cooperateurs integrated into the Basque communities.

Table 7.1 Willingness to transfer to firm

	Cooperateurs	%	Workers	%
Would transfer without monetary incentive	8	1	11	4
Would transfer with some monetary incentive (up to 50 per cent rise)	155	27	144	54
Would not transfer	398	71	113	42
Total	561	100	268	100

Chi-square$_2$ = 64.0: significant at 0.005.

Table 7.2 Willingness of cooperateurs to transfer to:

	Basque firm	%	Spanish cooperative	%
Would transfer for pay incentive (up to 50%)	163	29	185	34
Would not transfer	398	71	353	66
Total	561	100	538	100

Chi-square$_2$ = 3.6: significant at 0.06.

The location of a cooperative in a smaller or larger community would also be expected to affect the desire to withdraw capital. Subsamples within the cooperative group support this hypothesis as well. While 44 per cent of Mondragon-based respondents to the second questionnaires

Table 7.3 Desire to withdraw accumulated profits while working

		Yes	No	Total
		Desire for withdrawal		
Integration	Basque	342	376	718
	Non-Basque	113	66	179
	Total	455	442	897

Chi-square$_1$ = 13.8: significant at 0.005.

indicate a desire to withdraw accumulated profits, 67 per cent of the cooperateurs situated in larger industrial centers desired to do so. Basque and non-Basque proportions were similar in these two groups, but there are strong indications that the latter group feels less well-integrated into their cooperatives than does the former. Eighty-three per cent of the Mondragon-based sample had 'many' friends and relatives working in their enterprise, compared to only 47 per cent of the second group. Cooperateurs in large urban centers were more prepared to switch employment to other firms in response to hypothetical offers of higher pay. They were also strongly attracted to the cooperative by the prospect of work rather than the distinctive nature of the enterprise. In their attitudes to management and the Caja Laboral Popular, they appear to be less imbued with the cooperative ethic.

Small communities reinforce cooperative solidarity by minimizing the number of reference groups relative to whose status individual cooperateurs can compare themselves. A large environment is composed of a number of such reference groups with different lifestyles and standards of living which then are reflected in a diverse commercial environment. In larger communities, shops selling furs, antiques and imports line the same streets as those selling humbler goods. Diverse reference groups undermine cooperative solidarity especially when exit options are limited because disaffected members must be accommodated.

At the same time individual self interest has not been suppressed in Mondragon. It is most evident in the struggle over earnings differentials. Much as in a conventional firm, the lowest-paid cooperateurs desire a narrowing of differentials relative to those at higher levels: see Table 7.4. Without constraints on mobility Mondragon would stand to lose a greater proportion of its high-paid cooperateurs to other firms since these members are most vulnerable to market forces.

The problem of reconciling compressed differentials with market forces is most acute when vital technical specialists have to be imported

Table 7.4   Earnings and attitude to differentials

		\multicolumn{4}{c}{*Differentials should be:*}		
		Wider	*Same*	*Smaller*	*Total*
	Lowest paid	17	30	108	155
Earnings	Intermediate	44	77	85	206
Category	Highest paid	31	75	13	119
		92	182	206	480

Chi-square$_1$ = 97.2: significant at 0.005.

at market rates. Mondragon sometimes copes with this through consultancy and collaborative arrangements with outside firms. With short-term assignments these methods can be successful. It is sometimes hard to explain the need for highly specialized and paid foreign technicians and engineers, although accurate information on their necessity for solving problems can help the community to appreciate their importance. Difficulties mount if consultants become institutionalized in the cooperatives on a longer term basis. Once they become identified as part of the local community, this creates a distinct reference group and breaks solidarity.

Lower turnover in the Mondragon group leads to a pattern of joining dates different to that which would be expected in a conventional firm. Joining profiles differ in two important respects. Firstly, Mondragon's sustained, rapid expansion from a small base in the 1950s implies that few cooperateurs joined before 1960 relative to those in later years. Secondly, the control firms contain a larger proportion of transients than do the cooperatives. The joining-date distribution of the control group is bimodal, indicating a larger number of recent joiners despite the general economic slowdown after 1972. The cooperatives are not havens for casual or intermittent workers.

Lower intrinsic mobility of cooperateurs is advantageous. In its absence, maintaining managerial and specialist skills would prove a more severe problem. On the other hand, immobility and an emphasis on job security raise potential difficulties for the long-run coexistence of cooperatives with conventional capitalist enterprises. To cope with possible shifts in demand, the diverse product mix of Mondragon is essential to facilitate the transfer of labor between enterprises experiencing different fortunes. This is seen as a major safety valve by cooperative management. However, this option provides only a limited flexibility even to so well-developed a group as Mondragon, where market and technology change are currently forcing consideration of redundancy. Until recently, it was unthinkable to consider making cooperative members redundant, and the institutions to cope with such an eventuality did not even exist. Economic circumstances have enforced a reconsideration. By 1980, Lagun Aro was studying the possibility of introducing unemployment insurance. The extension of the central social agency to shoulder the expense of redundancy was seen as necessary to share the burden between the various cooperatives.

The impact on capital availability of making established workers redundant, or of higher labor turnover in general could be considerable. If sustained reinvestment of surplus into individual accounts is the main source of equity capital accumulation, long continuous spells of employment are necessary for high equity/man ratios, E. Thomas and Logan (1982) estimate the accumulation of capital in individual accounts for two hypothetical cooperateurs. The 'typical average' cooperateur starts with a work point index of 1.25 (on the scale 1–3). Over 20 years he works his way up to an index of 1.60. His accumulation of capital is roughly linear, from 99,000 pesetas to 1.9 million in current terms. The 'above average' cooperateur starts at 1.60 working up to an index of 2.90 by which time his equity reaches 3.4 million pesetas. The profile of accumulation (through revaluation and surplus distribution) is similar. Real equilibrium asset profiles may be computed, assuming away real capital gains and losses, by deflating nominal profiles by revaluation coefficients. It is then possible to estimate X_i; real equity holdings given length of stay for the typical average cooperateur, assuming Mondragon rules of surplus sharing.

There is of course no obligation to revalue capital when business conditions dictate otherwise. Take conditions over the past 20 years as representative. In the present exercise, no allowance is made for the approximate 20 per cent of surplus allocated to reserves in assessing the impact on the cooperative's capital base. The X_i are shown in Figure 7.1, together with four vintage profiles and resulting simulated values of E which depends on the vintage profile of the workforce.

L_1 represents a state of no growth with no labor attrition except through retirement after 22 years. L_2 is for steady growth at 10 per cent per annum. $E(L_2)$ is below $E(L_1)$ by 30 per cent. This indicates the conflict between two objectives of Mondragon: employment creation implies more younger workers and lower capital intensity. L_3 corresponds to the employment duration profile of our first survey. If attrition of the existing workforce can be held to zero and profitability can be maintained, the average equity/man can be kept constant during a transition to steady growth at 10 per cent per annum. It can rise considerably during a transition to slower steady growth, because the impact of retirement is more than compensated by the savings of the

Figure 7.1
Employment Duration and Equity Accumulation

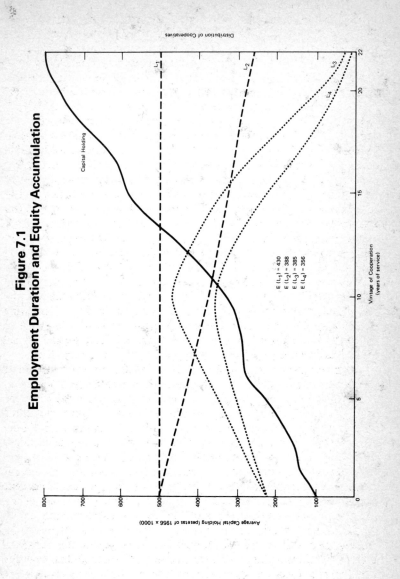

$E(L_1) = 430$
$E(L_2) = 388$
$E(L_3) = 385$
$E(L_4) = 356$

Capital Holding

L_1
L_2
L_3
L_4

Distribution of Cooperatives

Average Capital Holding (pesetas of 1956 × 1000)

Vintage of Cooperation
(years of service)

existing vintages of cooperateurs. Retirement itself should not pose a large problem for the Mondragon group, even if retirees are able to withdraw accumulated profits, as they are obliged to do in two years under present cooperative law.

In contrast, labor turnover presents a serious problem. We represent turnover simply by a steady rate of attrition, equal for workers of all vintages. Profile L_4 is based on L_3 but includes a 3 per cent annual attrition rate. E declines by 9 per cent. In balanced growth the vintage profile depends approximately on the sum of the growth and labor attrition rates. A one percentage point rise in either puts equal downwards pressure on E. A rise of 3 per cent in attrition thus needs to be offset by a similar fall in the growth rate to maintain the cooperative's capital intensity. It is difficult to grow without locking-in a cooperative work force for very substantial periods. If rapid growth creates opportunities for challenging work and so reduces the incidence of voluntary quits, the cooperative is subject to a destabilizing feedback. When favourably placed to expand it is easier to build up equity; in time of poor performance and low growth reinvestment may fall.

In summary, a number of obstacles limit the replicability of Mondragon-style cooperatives in densely industrialized society. To maintain incentives and encourage reinvestment of surplus it is necessary that a significant portion of the capital of a cooperative be owned by its individual cooperateurs. Changing conditions and technology render labor mobility desirable, to the extent that specialization gains are not outweighed by the absence of the 'exit' option as analyzed by Hirschman (1974). Perhaps more important is the preservation of individual choice in changing firms, location or occupation. Within a Mondragon-type system, a conflict appears between the three objectives: (a) high mobility, (b) equity accumulation, and (c) appropriately structured incentives for reinvestment of surplus. For communal, and perhaps ethnic, reasons, naturally low mobility of Mondragon cooperateurs has diminished the potential conflict between these objectives, permitting rapid growth and accumulation. The obstacles appear to be less serious when cooperatives are established in rural areas or for regional development.

8 Jobs – But Not For All

Virtually every organization screens prospective entrants by some set of criteria. Firms are no exception. Screening by conventional firms takes into account variables not strictly related to the task at hand. Blackburn and Mann (1979) emphasize selection of workers on conventional firms as being heavily influenced by criteria of obedience and regularity. The extensive pre-screening to enter schools feeding Japanese corporations was described in Chapter 3. Z firms are believed to screen entrants according to group acceptability.

Screening to enter Mondragon is of two kinds, social and financial. The group applies criteria specific to the cooperative form. In drawing up short lists of applicants the most important social variable is integration: both into the local community, and, potentially, into the cooperative. This carries high weight in assessing candidates:

> Once a person is inside he makes demands so we have to be very careful just who we select. Not only professional qualifications but morals are closely looked at. We concern ourselves about how the person behaves in the community. If he is bad, we put him on trial before allowing him to join our cooperative.[1]

Following acceptance a worker undergoes a trial period of some six months during which time foremen's reports again assess his social acceptability. Promotion also takes social variables into account, judging members on the degree to which they contribute to the co-operative spirit. 'Relational skills' are given a weight of 20 per cent in judging the rank of an individual cooperateur. While in the cooperative members are exposed to an extensive socialization process which includes courses in the cooperative ethic.

Monetary screening of potential entrants is effected by requiring a down payment, roughly equal to one year's earnings at the lowest level. A further screening is introduced by the knowledge that part of this and subsequent accumulated profits may be forfeited on premature departure. Sometimes part of the down payment can be borrowed from the

Caja, but a proportion must be paid in cash, on entry. If, for the average young Basque worker, such a down payment is perceived as a significant amount, monetary screening might result in a work force with characteristics different from those of the rest of the population. Unless the capital market works very well, past employment plays a large role in permitting a worker to join. An element of sacrifice is considered a necessary sign of the commitment of a new entrant. Cooperative employment may not be for all, especially for those most in need of jobs.

At the same time, cooperative success has increased the pool of potential applicants, just as successful firms are able to increase their recruiting pools by allocating part of their revenues to increasing wages and maintaining the promise of long-term security. Such elite employers can then select workers from chosen backgrounds. This institutionalizes the differences between workers in different firms and fragments the labor market into privileged and less privileged sectors. The less privileged sector will steadily become more dependent on the privileged sector for local purchasing of consumer goods, services and intermediates. But it may not be possible to sustain such a focal point of regional development without the screening process when this is needed for efficiency and competitiveness with industry outside the region.

Almost all our cooperative respondents considered their contribution as a fairly or very large sum to invest. In the eyes of the control group, the contribution is perceived as the prime barrier to joining, followed closely by the fear of being 'locked-in' and unable to withdraw capital. The capital requirement plausibly screens out a substantial number of lower-income applicants, just as potential locking-in would be expected to reduce applications by workers not seriously intending to stay. This was clearly a management objective, understandably so in view of the impact of turnover on average equity/man.

Table 8.1 compares the employment experience of cooperateurs and control group workers prior to their current job status. The higher proportion of previously unemployed in the control is probably associated, at least to some extent, with the capital requirement of Mondragon. A past history of unemployment or job instability may act as another screen to cooperative entrants.

Further evidence of screening is provided by Tables 8.2 and 8.3. Far more cooperateurs saw the cooperatives as one employment option out of a range of alternative opportunities. Correspondingly, relative to the control, they declared themselves to have been less motivated to join merely because of a desire for work. This impression is reinforced by the observation that 65 per cent of cooperateurs indicated that they would have refused a similar job on a local conventional firm had one

Table 8.1 **Prior employment status**

		Cooperatives	%	Firms	%	Total
			Enterprise of respondent			
Status	Employed before joining	687	67	122	44	809
	Unemployed before joining	341	33	151	56	492
	Total	1,028	100	273	100	1,301

Chi-square$_1$ = 45.0: significant at 0.005.

been offered. In spite of the deterrent posed by the capital contribution, they favored joining their cooperative. Relative to conventional firms, Mondragon has provided jobs to those not needing them. Job creation by the Mondragon group is thus largely indirect, through siphoning workers off other firms and through multiplier effects of rising local incomes.[2]

Table 8.2 **Alternative employment opportunities**

		Cooperatives	%	Firms	%	Total
			Enterprise of respondent			
Alternative employment opportunity	No	332	33	139	50	471
	Yes	675	67	137	50	812
	Total	1,007	100	276	100	1,283

Chi-square$_1$ = 28.2: significant at 0.005.

Table 8.3 **Main motivation for joining enterprise**

		Cooperatives	%	Firms	%	Total
			Enterprise of respondent			
Main motivation for joining	Cooperative/working conditions	628	65	61	23	689
	Employment	298	31	183	72	481
	Basque Enterprise	40	4	11	4	51
	Total	966	100	255	100	1,221

Chi-square$_2$ = 146.1: significant at 0.005.

What evidence exists that screening might contribute to lower industrial conflict on the cooperatives by maintaining consensus? Rigorous formulation and testing of any such relationship must be approached with caution for several reasons. How can we measure 'cooperative attitudes' or the circumstances under which individuals joined? Both dependent and independent variables are multifaceted, subjective amalgams. Additionally, the sample of cooperateurs is necessarily limited to those selected. It is not possible to sample those failing to enter, and even if it were, members of a control group could not be expected to comment credibly on a work situation they had not experienced. The non-representative distribution of cooperateurs over characteristics can bias estimated relationships rather severely.

For each composite variable a number of responses were selected to represent various facets. Multiple regressions were performed between each facet of the dependent variable – attitudes – and the independent explanatory variable – circumstances of joining. Each regression included a set of standardizing variables to take into account the possible influences of third variables correlated with dependent variables. Let:

Y_i = facet of cooperative attitudes where $i = 1, 2, \ldots 7$
X_j = facet of joining condition where $j = 1, 2, 3, 4$
S_k = standardizing variable k where $k = 1, \ldots 7$

Each regression takes the form:

$$Y_i = a_{ij}X_j + \sum_{k=1}^{7} b_{ij}S_k$$

assuming linear relationships. The facets of cooperative attitudes and joining conditions are:[3]

Y_1 = Perception of greater job control;
Y_2 = Perceived degree of participation in important decisions;
Y_3 = Ability to voice opinions or complaints;
Y_4 = Perceived distance between cooperative workers and mánagement;
Y_5 = View of the Caja Laboral as acting in workers' interests;
Y_6 = Opinion on need for trade unions in cooperative;
Y_7 = Desire to withdraw shareholding from cooperative;
X_1 = Willingness to have taken similar job outside cooperative;
X_2 = Perception on joining cooperative as only employment opportunity;
X_3 = Declared principal motive for joining cooperative;
X_4 = Whether in employment before joining cooperative.

Standardizing variables included are: age, sex, Basqueness, joining date, wage, occupation, and 'ideology'. The last variable is proxied by perceptions of the role of management on conventional Basque firms.

Decisions on whether a candidate is acceptable are probably influenced by a set of variables which includes our variables X_1–X_4, so that empirical results will be affected by worker selection biases. Perfect screening over these variables would be expected to result in not merely orthogonal, but compensating variations between the X_i and between the Y_i. For example, to be acceptable, a prospective worker, if currently unemployed, might be required to demonstrate greater co-operative motivation than one employed, since the latter is, *prima facie*, more likely to be joining out of an acceptable cooperative impulse. Similarly, attitudes favourable and unfavorable to cooperativism would tend to offset, rather than reinforce each other. The estimated a $_{ij}$ would then be expected not to be significant and to have random sign. Perfect screening may therefore be tested by looking for compensating, rather than reinforcing variations between different entry variables and different attitudinal variables; an individual should not register dissatisfaction on *all* counts.[4] It should also be reflected in an absence of relationships between the two sets of variables.

Correlation matrices between the independent and dependent variable facets are shown in Tables 8.4 and 8.5 respectively. Correlations are low, yet generally statistically significant. More importantly, all signs for the X_i are as would be predicted in the absence of screening and only two nonsignificant correlations between the Y_j differ from the pattern. The X_i and Y_j components do indeed exhibit some common directionality although dispersion about their common direction is large.

Table 8.6 shows the matrix of regression coefficients a$_{ij}$ as obtained from the twenty-eight regressions. Coefficients are small, yet sixteen out of twenty-eight are significant at the 5 per cent level and the signs of twenty-three coefficients (including all sixteen significant ones) are

Table 8.4 X_i correlation matrix

	X_1	X_2	X_3	X_4
X_1	1			
X_2	0.24*	1		
X_3	−0.46*	−0.24*	1	
X_4	−0.35*	−0.10*	0.30*	1

* Significant at 1 per cent level.

consistent with the hypothesis that attitudes towards the cooperative
relate systematically to the circumstances under which individuals join.
Broadly speaking, individuals seeing the cooperative as one of a range
of employment possibilities, hence less dependent on it for a job,
exhibit more cooperative attitudes. Interpret coefficients as probabilities.[5] Then, for example, suppose that 100 workers were to join the
cooperatives as a last resort for jobs. Compared to 100 workers joining
with alternative options of employment, some sixteen extra would
perceive a serious division between management and workers.

Table 8.5 Y_j correlation matrix

	Y_1	Y_2	Y_3	Y_4	Y_5	Y_6	Y_7
Y_1	1						
Y_2	0.16*	1					
Y_3	−0.13*	−0.26*	1				
Y_4	0.10*	−0.06**	0.30*	1			
Y_5	0.19*	0.19*	−0.14*	−0.25*	1		
Y_6	−0.07	0.02**	0.11*	0.11*	−0.02	1	
Y_7	−0.06	−0.10*	0.14*	0.19*	−0.13*	0.07	1

* Significant at 1 per cent level.
** Sign inconsistent with common directionality.

Table 8.6   Regression coefficients a_{ij}

		Index i			
		1	*2*	*3*	*4*
	1	−0.13*	0.04**	0.13*	0.09*
	2	−0.05	−0.12	0.24*	0.24*
	3	0.05	0.11*	−0.07	−0.10*
Index j	4	0.13*	0.16*	−0.13*	0.04**
	5	−0.06*	0.05**	0.07*	0.10*
	6	0.06	0.10*	−0.10*	0.07**
	7	0.03	0.13*	−0.06	0.05**

* Significant at 5 per cent level.
** Inconsistent sign.

It is not possible to form unbiased estimates of the relationship
between characteristics and attitudes which would prevail with a less

rigorous selection policy. However, the effect of selection is, as noted above, to bias the regression coefficients towards zero. Estimates therefore understate true values, providing lower bounds on the strength of interactions with a less rigorous selection policy. Attempts to expand the cooperatives unduly rapidly, or to emphasize the objective of direct job creation (the offering of employment to individuals less able to find work in conventional firms), would probably result in a considerable weakening of their present ideological solidarity.

9　The Contribution of Mondragon

Mondragon spans a unique divide in that it is able to suggest solutions to pressing problems in both industrialized and developing countries. To realize this potential will require an innovative approach on the part of policy makers and careful assessment of whether local conditions fit the requirements of the cooperative option. How Mondragon comes through the 1980s will be the ultimate test of the experiment.

In the industrialized economies the tradeoff between incomes and efficiency is tightening with slower growth. There is increased recognition of the limits to expansionary demand–management with structural supply constraints. This has led to interest in alternatives to traditional confrontational collective bargaining on the part of industry. It has also led to some acknowledgement by unions that aggressive collective bargaining may be appropriate at some stages of capitalist development but is sometimes counterproductive. The discipline of industrial relations has been slow to adjust to the growing need for analysis based on a more unitary model of the firm. Mondragon is of interest from the viewpoint of industrial regeneration and for regional development. If anything, adversarial labor relations now accelerate capital flight and economic decline.

Mondragon addresses economic concerns of developing countries: growth, rapid capital and skill accumulation and employment creation. It also stands for a third option of considerable appeal, between capitalism and state-directed socialism. Many developing countries have experimented with industrial and agricultural cooperatives, frequently with poor results because political concerns have supplanted economic considerations. Mondragon suggests that, properly implemented, the cooperative option can do better.

As a worker cooperative Mondragon is unique; as a consensus firm it is one of many, a little closer to the Japanese than to the Western model, but with distinctive methods of maintaining solidarity. It may be no more difficult to replicate than to transplant the Japanese model of industrial relations since the latter has its roots in a distinctive culture. Mondragon relies on a structure of asset ownership which should be replicable in quite a wide variety of circumstances. Having worker shareholders relaxes the need for other methods of building consensus which may require time and considerable attitudinal change. Individual-account worker ownership is quite compatible with capitalism.

Survey results suggest a generally good, though not perfect, climate of labor relations in the cooperatives, and a close link between consensus and productivity. This confirms the possibility, established by studies in the United States, of efficient cooperative organization. Productivity is raised in two ways: lower resistance to hierarchical control because of high-trust relationships, and informal support between members at the same level. Even strict discipline may not be viewed unfavourably because members are involved with their firm. Mondragon suggests a very limited role for trade unions in true cooperatives, along the lines of enterprise unionism in Japan.

Because of the conflict between three objectives: capital accumulation, labor instability and solidarity through compressed differentials, the Mondragon model seems best suited to reindustrialization, or developing isolated areas with stable communities. It may serve as a catalyst for regional development or regeneration. Small communities help to maintain consensus. They partially insulate cooperatives from pressures of the external labor market and other reference groups, and help to permit a more compressed wage payments scale. Communal attachment helps to retain capital within the enterprise by reducing the desire to remit savings to distant areas. Low labor turnover is crucial for building cooperative equity in individual accounts. Cooperative survival may not be possible in a fluid labor market. Cooperatives may not be best in industries where rapid technical change requires personnel to be turned over frequently. Communal capital holdings may allow compressed differentials to be reconciled with labor mobility, but at a high cost. Individual shareholdings appear to play an important motivating role at Mondragon. Communalized capital lowers efficiency and shortens horizons.

Strong local attachments also are important in preserving managerial talent. Mondragon suggests less capital–labor conflict, but that managers face a critical internal audience of worker–owners. This prevents the growth of managerial X-inefficiency and a bloated management structure, but, when combined with compressed differentials, has the cost of constraining the pool of potential managers.

Finally, cooperative membership may not be for everyone. In particular, the converting of a conventional firm with minimal socialization of its existing staff into the cooperative ethic is not likely to result in an enduring cooperative. Screening is probably important in providing Mondragon with a distinctive pool of workers. These appear more likely to support the cooperative ethic and maintain solidarity with fellow cooperateurs. Mondragon's reputation permits it to recruit members with more favorable employment histories. As alternative opportunities shrink, the pool of potential cooperateurs grows, to include more individuals viewing the cooperatives primarily as a job opportunity. Unless screening is perfect, greater pressure is placed on the socialization process after entry to maintain consensus. Recognizing the importance of the process, Mondragon devotes considerable resources to educating its members in the cooperative ideal.

Appendix: A Simple Model of Motivation and Control

Production possibilities for output y are assumed to be given by a *production function*

$$y = f(\overline{k}, \ell_1, \ldots, \ell_n) \qquad (1)$$

with f concave, displaying non-increasing returns given fixed capital $\overline{k}$. ℓ_j represents labor (effort) input of worker j. This is broadly defined to include punctuality, cooperation, furthering work quality and so forth. We abstract from risk, but assume that some effort is required to monitor ℓ_j, possibly above some minimal level.

Worker Activities and Environment: Worker j has two activities, labor ℓ_j and monitoring (encouragement, control) $c_j \geq 0$. Given his environment he attempts to maximize a separable, individualistic utility function:

$$\max_{c_j \ell_j} u_j(m_j \ell_j c_j) = m_j - u_2(\ell_j) - u_3(c_j) \qquad (2)$$

where m_j is his monetary reward, u is concave and

$$m_j = \lambda_j f \text{ where } \sum_{j=1}^{n} \lambda_j = 1 \qquad (3)$$

Decision on $[\lambda_j]$ is *profit sharing rule*.

Worker j's *environment* γ_j sets the divergence between the marginal disutility of labor and the reward accruing to j from greater overall profitability: by (2), (3) maximization yields

$$u_2' = \lambda_j \frac{\partial f}{\partial \ell_j} + \gamma_j \qquad (4)$$

where $\gamma_j = \gamma_j(c_1, \ldots, c_{j-1}, c_{j+1}, \ldots, c_n)$ is a function of $\qquad (5)$
the behavior of other workers and managers. Linearizing:

$$\gamma_j = \sum_k A_{jk} c_k \qquad (6)$$

where $A_{kk} = 0$ for all k. We may now write:

$$A_{jk} = G_{jk}H_{jk} \qquad (7)$$

where G_{jk} represents the *power* (moral, legal, etc.) of k over the actions of j and H_{jk} the *observation potential* of j by k. Together $A_{jk} = G_{jk}H_{jk}$ is the *control matrix* of the enterprise.

Interpretation of (4) is that monitoring by others may 'encourage' or 'force' greater effort out of j than he would deliver if only motivated by his share of profits. There are no natural units for measuring monitoring intensity. Therefore it is here expressed directly in terms of the 'wedge' between marginal utility u_2' and the own-profit increment. This wedge relates to monitoring efforts $[c_k]$ through A, which is made up of two elements.[1]

A Special Case: Production and Informational Symmetry. Suppose that (i) f is symmetric in ℓ_i and ℓ_j for all i and j, and displays decreasing returns; (ii) that all utility functions are identical and concave, and $u_2'(0)$, $u_3'(0) = 0$; and (iii) that for all j, k, j = k, $A_{jk} = $ constant $= 1$; (iv) n given; and (v) $\Sigma\ell_i = \ell$. If we omit the influence of γ_i in (4), the problem of choosing the optimal $[\lambda_j]$ to maximize output is straightforward: by (4), concavity and symmetry of u_2 and f_ℓ, $\ell = \Sigma \ell_j$ is maximized when $\lambda_j = \frac{1}{n}$ for all j. Also, by symmetry, $\ell_j = \ell/n$.

Therefore, equal profit sharing results both in greatest aggregate ℓ and its optimal distribution because of diminishing returns.

However, with larger n any influence of profit sharing becomes insignificant because of (4) becoming $u_2' = \frac{1}{n} \frac{\partial f}{\partial \ell_j}$. As $n \to \infty$, effort levels decline to minimal levels because of the 'free rider' problem.

Allowing now for the influence of controls γ_j: by symmetry, $\gamma_j = \sum_{k \neq j} c_k$. Let $\gamma = \sum_j \gamma_j$. With equal distribution of surplus $\gamma = (n-1)\sum_j c_j$. By symmetry and concavity of u and f, the output-maximizing solution will still be the symmetric one $\lambda_j = \frac{1}{n}$. At this solution γ may not be maximized relative to its value for alternative distributions $[\lambda_j]$, although (a) $\ell = \sum_j \ell_j$ will be, and (b) the distribution of ℓ over workers will again be equal and optimal. The curvature of individual utility functions could be such that the direct incentive effect described above almost suffices to extract maximum 'possible' effort. Individualistic 'self-discipline' could substantially replace discipline imposed by a

---

[1] In principle the elements of A (and their impact on individuals) could be made to depend explicitly on the cooperative 'ethic' rather than purely on the structure of financial incentives. Evidence from Mondragon cannot easily separate these effects because of the correlation between capital holdings and length of stay, itself plausibly correlated with 'socialization' into cooperative society. As noted above, it seems unwise to found arguments for cooperatives solely on the presumption of fundamental changes in economic man.

hierarchy or by peer pressure. Whether this is likely in a large organization depends on the prevailing view of self-discipline and, no doubt, on the 'backup' of effective peer pressure. From inside a successful cooperative 'discipline' might thus not be perceived as extreme. From outside, perceptions based mainly on productivity and on 'objective' criteria (such as incidence of strikes, absenteeism) would tend to see a more disciplined environment.

Asymmetries: The above model provides a framework for analyzing the effects of real-world asymetries or scale economies at individual task level, so permitting an assessment of the gains or losses from wider distribution of the surplus. Asymmetries or scale economies can enter in several ways: through production functions f, utility functions u, power coefficients G, or observation coefficients H. Omitting, for simplicity, differences in u, the model suggests two reasons for extending incentives to an individual j, the *direct* incentive of greater reward and the *indirect* incentive to encourage others a little more for greater reward. The more tightly an individual can be controlled by others and the less control or influence he can exert over others, the less is the argument for extending control incentives. The less he can be controlled by others and the more the use of his own 'discretion' matters to the enterprise, the more argument for extending incentives (according to the direct argument), considering individualistic decision-making alone. Incentives must, therefore, be extended to: (a) certain (probably white-collar) workers with wide discretion, and whose tasks are difficult to monitor (managers perhaps, or certain key professionals). For such a worker j, $\sum_k A_{jk}$ is small, but $\frac{\partial f}{\partial \ell_j}$ large. And (b) workers with discretionary monitoring ability: for worker j if over a wide range of i, A_{ij} is large (or $\sum_i A_{ij}$ large). This implies both (a) good opportunities to *observe* and (b) the *power* and *influence* to use observation ability to persuade.

Both technology and social environment affect the optimal incentive pattern. Suppose good instruments for observation permit a few managers to assess the performance of most of the workforce. This argues for concentration of incentives. However, if the political or social environment is such that managers cannot in fact *enforce* or *persuade*, the argument is far weaker; $\sum_i H_{ij}$ may be large, but $\sum_i G_{ij}$ small. An example might perhaps be the case of British industry in the 1970s with the rise of the shop-floor movement. There may then be an argument for spreading incentives to workers with lower H_{ij}s but with the ability to change the 'rules' to permit higher G_{ij} to be achieved.

The Role of Consensus: Developing High-Trust Relationships. Suppose the barriers to efficiency are not the H_{ij}s but the G_{ij}s. While the H_{ij}s are perhaps fairly exogenous (observation potential depends on technology) the G_{ij} depend on the generally accepted power structure. One reason to extend incentives broadly is to try to raise the G_{ij}s generally, by establishing a broader consensus on the need for control. This is necessary to prevent the blocking of management initiatives by nonmanagerial employees, who must be convinced that productivity gains are in their interest rather than the forerunners to redundancy.

Monetary incentives to management may, therefore, be lower on a cooperative. This may however be compensated by far higher Gs. Management exists to control and monitor because of technology which dictates that some individuals have higher H_{ij}s. In the interests of the collective, these control as its delegated authority, but consensus prevents the growth of informal agreements and formal regulations which tend, over time, to lower the power coefficients G.

Notes

Chapter 1 Footnotes

1. 'Reindustrialization' has been the subject of studies although the concept is still imperfectly defined because it is not clear how far and in what sectors optimal industrialization would proceed. An extensive discussion for the US is in *Business Week* (1980). Another clear statement of the problem associated with the impending loss of the manufacturing base of the Northeast is due to Rohatyn (1980) who also puts forward suggestions to rebuild industry. For a more radical statement – and prescription, see Rifkin and Barber (1978) who emphasize the redirection of pension funds towards this end. This subject is addressed in the British context in Blackaby (1979).
2. There have also been trends towards employee buyouts in Canada and France. For a survey see Bradley and Gelb (1983). For British examples, such as National Freight, see *Financial Times Survey*, October 30, 1981.
3. For a review of legislation at national level involving cooperatives see Bradley and Gelb (1983) Chapter V. For the *Massachusetts Employee Cooperative Act* see House of Representatives Record No. 6137, May 4, 1982.
4. See Bradley and Hill (1983).
5. Jorgensen and Nishimizu (1978).
6. Cadbury and Rowntree are two prominent examples.
7. See Swift (1975) for discussion of the flight from unionism.
8. For a brief description and appraisal of ESOPs see Select Committee on Small Business (1979).
9. This is discussed in Bradley and Gelb (1983). Chapter V. Senator Russell Long (1983) provides an eloquent statement.

Chapter 2 Footnotes

1. *Liga de Education: Estatisticas del Alto Deva Curso 1976, 1977*, as quoted in Thomas and Logan (1982), p. 65.
2. Thomas and Logan (1982), p. 111 provide data until 1979. The economic downturn of the 1980s has had a depressing effect on the profitability of the cooperatives as it has on that of conventional firms.
3. The distribution formula is as follows: let R_1 = net profits and R_2 = total payroll costs (wages and interest income). Then the total proportion of profits to individual accounts is $P = R_2/(R_1 + R_2)$. P is also constrained to be not more than 60 per cent of R_2 and not more than 70 per cent of R_1. Similar formulae apply to losses. For descriptions of the formulae and their applications see Oakeshott (1978) and Thomas and Logan (1982).
4. Blackburn and Mann (1979).

5. Interview with Ulgor Management, July 1979.
6. Mondragon's rules have influenced a number of associations dedicated to promoting worker cooperatives. The Massachusetts-based Industrial Cooperatives Association (ICA) has been particularly concerned to replicate the organization of the Group.

Chapter 3 Footnotes

1. Jones (1980) examines the extent to which Mondragon rules differ from those of other Western 'cooperatives' and satisfy the Vanek criteria.
2. Between 1801 and 1821 the populations of Birmingham, Glasgow, Liverpool, Manchester and Nottingham grew by 132%, whereas, for the country as a whole, the population increase was 52%. This phase is described by Babbage (1832) p. 6. Industrialization, however, had not penetrated all areas. Approximately half the population still lived in rural areas as late as 1850.
3. Owen, (1816) p. 50. Owen was associated with the New Lanark Mills for 25 years. However, the concern here is with a period between 1800 and 1813 which Cole, (1925) describes as: 'a time of quiet hard work during which New Lanark was gradually transformed into the most successful establishment of the day in its human as well as its commercial results.' p. 745.
4. *Ibid*, p. 34.
5. Owen, (1816a) p. 13.
6. Cole, (1925) *op. cit.*, p. 78.
7. *Ibid*, pp. 74–5.
8. Owen, (1817) *Report to the committee for the Relief of the Manufacturing Poor* quoted in Beer (1929) p. 164.
9. Education is believed to generally have a high payoff to developing countries. For a discussion of the role of human resource development see *World Bank* (1980).
10. See Harrison, (1969) p. 155.
11. *Ibid*, p. 154.
12. Thompson (1963) p. 780.
13. See, eg, Hill (1981).
14. Edwards (1979) provides a vivid analysis of the increasing contradiction between hierarchy and efficient control in contemporary capitalist environments. For a discussion of the role of trust relationships in production see Fox (1974).
15. As would be expected, working conditions differ between cooperatives and are usually more pleasant on newer ones. Eaton (1979) describes the 'sweat shop' environment of certain cooperatives. This may be misleading since the control and representation systems are so different to those in exploitative capitalist firms.
16. We judge Mondragon to be close to the Japanese model in characteristics 3, 4, 5, 9, 10, 11, and 16; to the A firm in 7, 8, 14; distinctive or an intermediate mixture in the remainder.

Chapter 4 Footnotes

1. The logistic difficulties presented by large-scale interviewing, together with Basque reluctance to discuss sensitive points with outsiders biased us towards surveys. These, in addition, are able to take advantage of the high level of literacy achieved in the Basque country.
2. To ask the control for perceptions of Mondragon is preferable to cross-checking in reverse because of the possibly self-selecting nature of the cooperateurs. The control, it may be fairly assumed, is more likely to include respondents unsympathetic to Mondragon (because they have not joined), hence likely to judge the cooperatives harshly.

Chapter 5 Footnotes

1. The concept of X-inefficiency was introduced by Leibenstein (1966).
2. A comparative perspective on the US and Europe on legislation, including Italy, is provided in Leveson and Wheeler (1980).
3. *Congressional Record*, 25 August PE3328, 1978.
4. For example, Vermont Asbestos experienced a dramatic turnaround when asbestos prices soared; but solidarity at Rath Meatpacking suffered through extreme adverse market pressure.
5. For a discussion see Woodward (1965, 1970).
6. In one study cited by Frieden (1979) only about 20 per cent of blue-collar workers agreed that they would benefit from greater productivity. In the long run, whether labor as a whole benefits depends on whether the output-increasing effect of greater productivity exceeds the depression of the real wage if innovation is labor-saving.
7. Society where production is organized along Mondragon lines is not classless at a point in time on the criterion of ownership since older cooperateurs own more capital, hence 'employ' younger cooperateurs. Except for the inclusion of interest in earnings used to distribute surplus it is classless from the viewpoint of extracting surplus value since this is not allocated on the basis of capital ownership.
8. For British union attitudes to alternative channels of worker representation see *Industrial Democracy* (1974).
9. Long (1979), Stern (1978).
10. Surveys of 50 Mondragon managers were conducted by Chris Clamp in July–October 1982. These observations draw on her work.

Chapter 6 Footnotes

1. This total is lower than previous totals because an error in the first questionnaire could have confused some respondents and therefore might have invalidated some replies. The discarded observations nevertheless, conform to the above pattern.
2. Interview with Mondragon manager, July 1979.
3. Thomas and Logan, *op. cit.*, pp. 49–52.
4. Interview with Director of the Entrepreneurial Division, Caja Laboral Popular, July 1979.
5. Williamson (1978), Marris and Wood (1971) discuss the various objectives of corporate management.

Chapter 7 Footnotes

1. Thomas and Logan (1982) and Oakeshott (1978) comment on distinctive features of Basque culture which are congruent with cooperatives.
2. Logan and Gregory (1981).
3. An example of village development in Sri Lanka may serve to illustrate the point. To improve market access a self-help program was initiated to build a road linking the village with the nearest highway. The road would however need to pass over the fields of the largest landowner, who opposed the project (partly because this would undermine his control on marketing). Without confronting the landlord, the organizers induced the villagers to build the road anyway, but it stopped at his boundary and continued on the other side. After some months of hard labor the road was completed – in full. With the symbolic unfinished road, the landlord had recognized that in order to remain part of the community it would be necessary to concede the right-of-way. This example is taken from the experience of the Sarvodaya movement. Sarvodaya is outlined in World Bank (1980).
4. Jamestown is described in *Community at Work* (1977), Meek and Whyte (1980).
5. Mondragon has considered departing from this principle to the extent that retirees are not paid out but receive a pension instead. They then become bearers of residual

risk however, without any voice in the operation of the enterprises on which they depend.

6. Interview with Caja Laboral Popular Manager, July 1979.

Chapter 8 Footnotes

1. Interview with founder member of Mondragon, July 1979.

2. The possible effect of third variables between sample and control which contribute to the different profiles in Tables 8.1, 8.2 and 8.3 does not undermine the screening argument since such variations are themselves probably the result of screening. For example, Mondragon may employ fewer females because these are more likely to want temporary employment or have less access to funds. Neither is the different pattern of joining dates between the cooperatives and control responsible.

3. These are regarded as different facets rather than as constituting a set of variables scaleable according to some criterion such as that of Guttman. There is no reason, for example, to believe that a positive answer to X_1 should imply a similar response to X_2 but that a positive X_2 need not imply positive X_1. All estimation is by ordinary least squares.

4. Individuals may be considered to possess a characteristic vector $z = (X_1, X_2, X_3)$ where X_1 and X_2 provide indications of ideological commitment, and X_3 denotes other attributes such as skills. The X_3 are distributed over the population of potential cooperative workers and selection involves choosing workers for whom $f(X_1X_2X_3) \geq k$ where k is some cutoff score. Positive correlation between X_1 and X_2 in the population will be negatively biased by selection, the bias being stronger the higher is k and the more weight is placed on X_1 and X_2 relative to other variables. For an indication of possible bias, let X_1 and X_2 each take value 1 and 0 with probability 0.5 and be positively correlated with coefficient 0.6. For simplicity, omit the influence of X_3. If 40 per cent are rejected by screening, correlation between X_1 and X_2 for the selected workers is -0.2. Screening changes the sign of *ex post* observed correlation from its value in the population of all workers.

5. Interpretation of regression coefficients as probabilities is appropriate in the case of dichotomous dependent variables. To avoid the problems of probabilities falling outside the (0, 1) range, logit or similar transformations may be used. Two of the seven dependent variables are trichotomous variables: for these, simple linear scaling (constant interval) has been used.

Bibliography

Aguren, S., *et al.* (1976), *The Volvo Kalma Plant*, SAF–LO, Stockholm.

Aho, M. and Orr, J. (1980), 'Demographic and Occupational Characteristics of Workers in Trade–Sensitive Industries', US Department of Labor Discussion Paper 2, Washington, D.C.

Babbage, C. (1835), *On the Economy of Machinery and Manufacture*, London.

Beer, M. (1929), *A History of British Socialism*, Bell and Sons, London.

Bell, D. (1962), *The End of Ideology*, The Free Press, New York.

Berman, K. (1967), 'The Industrial Context', in Coates, K. (ed.) (1976), *The New Worker Cooperatives*, Spokesman, Nottingham.

Blackaby, F. (ed.) (1979), *De-Industrialization*, Heinemann Educational Books, London.

Blackburn, R. and Mann, M., (1979), *The Working Class in the Labour Market*, Cambridge University Press.

Bradley, K. (1983), 'Age and Vintage Effects on Employee Workplace Attitudes', paper presented at the Work Organization Seminar, Dpt of Economics, University of Warwick.

Bradley, K. and Gelb, A. (1983), *Worker Capitalism: The New Industrial Relations*, Heinemann and MIT Press.

Bradley, K. and Hill, S. (1983), ' "After Japan": the Quality Circle Transplant and Productive Efficiency', *British Journal of Industrial Relations*, November.

Braverman, H. (1974), *Labor and Monopoly Capital*, Monthly Review Press, New York.

Business Week (1980), 'Reindustrialization', June.

Campbell, A., Keen, C., Norman G., and Oakeshott, R. (1977), *Workers Owners: the Mondragon Achievement*, Anglo–German Foundation, London.

Cole, G.D.H. (1925), *Robert Owen*, London.

Community at Work (1977) 'The Five Year Report of the Jamestown Area Labor–Management Committee', Jamestown.

Conte, M. and Tannenbaum, A.B. (1978), 'Employee-Owned Companies: Is the Difference Measurable?', *Monthly Labor Review*, July.

Dore, R. (1973), *British Factory, Japanese Factory*, Allen and Unwin, London.

Eaton, J. (1979), 'The Basque Workers' Cooperatives', *Journal of Industrial Relations*, vol. 10, no. 3, pp. 32–40.

Edwards, R. (1979), *Contested Terrain*, Basic Books, New York.

Fox, A. (1974), *Beyond Contract: Work, Power and Trust Relations*, Faber, London.

Frieden, K. (1979), *Productivity and Worker Participation*, National Center for Economic Alternatives, Washington, D.C.

Gaskell, (1836), *Artisans and Manufacturing: The Moral and Physical Conditions of the Manufacturing Population Considered with Reference to Mechanical Substitutes for Human Labour*, London.

Goldthorpe, J., Lockwood, D., Blechhofer, F. and Platt, J. (1968) and (1969), *The Affluent Worker Study*, 3 Volumes, Cambridge University Press.

Golt, S. (1980), 'The New Protectionism', in Leveson and Wheeler (eds.) (1980).

Gorrono, I. (1975), *Experiencia Cooperative en el Pais Vasco*, Durango, Leopoldo Zugaza.

Harrison, J.F.C. (1969), *Robert Owen and the Owenites in Britain and America*, Routledge and Kegan Paul, London.

Hill, S. (1981), *Competition and Control at Work: The New Industrial Sociology*, Heinemann, London.

Hirschman, A. (1970), *Exit Voice and Loyalty*, Harvaard University Press.

Hobsbawm, E.J. (1968), *Industry and Empire*, Weidenfeld and Nicolson, London.

Hufbauer, G.C. (1970), 'The Impact of National Characteristics and Technology on the Commodity Composition of the Trade in Manufactured Goods' in Vernon, R. (ed.), *The Technology Factor in International Trade*, NBER.

Industrial Democracy (1974): A statement of the Policy by the Trades Union Congress, TUC, London.

Jay, P. (1977), 'The Workers' Cooperative Economy', *Transactions of the Manchester Statistical Society*, pp. 1–43.

Johnson, A.G. and Whyte, W.F. (1977), 'The Mondragon System of Worker Producer Cooperatives', *Industrial and Labor Relations Review*, vol. 31, no. 1.

Jones, D.C. (1980), 'Producer Cooperatives in Industrialized Western Economies', *British Journal of Industrial Relations*, July.

Jorgensen, D.W. and Nishimizu, M. (1978), 'US and Japanese Economic Growth: 1952–1974: An International Comparison', *Economic Journal*, 88 (December), pp. 707–726.

Kornhauser, A., (1965), *The Mental Health of the Industrial Worker*, John Wiley, New York.

Lane, T. and Roberts, K. (1971), *Strike at Pilkington*, Fontana.

Leibenstein, H. (1966), 'Allocative Efficiency versus X-Efficiency', *American Economic Review*, June.

Leveson, I. and Wheeler, J. (eds.) (1980), *Western Economies in Transition: Structural Change and Adjustment Policies in Industrial Countries*, Westview Press, Colorado and Croom Helm, London.

Levine, A.L. (1967), *Industrial Retardation in Britain 1880–1914*, Weidenfeld and Nicolson, London.

Logan, C. and Gregory, D. (1981), *Cooperation and Job Creation in Wales: A Feasibility Study*, Report to the Welsh TUC, August.

Long, R.J. (1982), 'Employee Ownership: A Political History', Address delivered to the Conference on Employee Participation, Ownership and Management, John F. Kennedy School of Government, Harvard University, April 17.

Long, R.J. (1979), 'Employee Ownership and Attitudes Towards the Union', *Industrial Relations Industrielles*, vol. 33, no. 2.

Mann, M. (1973), *Consciousness and Action among the Western Working Class*, Macmillan.

Marris, R. and Wood, A. (1971) (eds.), *The Corporate Economy*, Macmillan, London.

Marsh, R.M. and Mannari, H. (1976), *Modernization and the Japanese Factory*, Princeton University Press.

Meek, C., and Whyte, W.F. (1980), 'The Jamestown Model of Cooperative Problem Solving,' Cornell University (mimeo).

McKenzie R. and Silver, A. (1968), *Angels in Marble: Working Class Conservatism in Urban England*, Heinemann Educational Books, London.

Miliband, R. (1969), *The State in Capitalist Society*, Merlin, London.

Moorhouse, H.F. (1976), 'Attitudes to Class and Class Relationships in Britain', *Sociology*.

Morishima, M. (1982), *Why Has Japan 'Succeeded'? Western Technology and the Japanese Ethics*, Cambridge University Press.

Nelson, D. (1975), *Managers and Workers*, Madison, Wisconsin.

Nelson, R. (1980), 'Technical Advance and Productivity Growth: Retrospect, Prospect, and Policy Issues', in Leveson and Wheeler (eds.) (1980).

Newby, H. (1977), *The Deferential Worker*, Allen and Unwin, London.

Nichols, T. (1969), *Ownership, Control and Ideology*, London.

Oakeshott, R. (1978), *The Case for Worker Coops*, Routledge and Kegan Paul, London.

Ohlin, G. (1978), 'Subsidies and Other Industrial Aids', in Warnecke, S.J. *et al.*, *International Trade and Industrial Policies*, Macmillan, London.

Ouchi, W. (1982), *Theory Z: How American Business can Meet the Japanese Challenge*, Avon, New York.

Owen, R. (1819), 'Address to the Inhabitants of New Lanark at the opening of the Institution established for the Foundation of Character,' London.

Owen, R. (1816), A New View of Society: Essays on the Formation of the Human Character.

Rifkin, J. and Barber, R. (1978), *The North Will Rise Again: Pensions, Politics and Power in the 1980s*, Beacon Press, Boston.

Rohatyn, F. (1980), 'The State of the Nation's Industry – All Talk and No Action', *Washington Post*, July 20.

Rothschild-Whitt, J. (1979), 'The Collective Organization: An Alternative to Rational-Bureaucratic Models', *American Sociological Review*, 44, Aug.

Select Committee on Small Business: US Senate (1979), *The Role of the Federal Government and Employee Ownership of Business*, U.S. Government Printing Office, Washington, D.C., March 20.

Stern, R.M. (1978), 'The Union Under Employee Ownership', paper presented at the 1978 Meeting of the American Psychological Association, Toronto, Canada.

Swift, R.A. (1975), *The NLRB and Management Decision Making*, IRU, University of Pennsylvania.

Thompson, E.P. (1963), *The Making of the English Working Class*, Gollancz, London.

Thornley, J. (1981), *Worker Cooperatives: Jobs and Dreams*, Heinemann Educational Books, London.

Thurow, L. (1981), 'Death by a Thousand Cuts', *New York Review of Books*, November 17, pp. 3–4.

Webb, S.B. (1921), *Consumers' Cooperatives Movement*, Longman, Green and Company, London.

Westergaard, J. (1970), 'The Rediscovery of the Cash Nexus', in Miliband, R. and Saville, J. (eds.), *The Socialist Register*, Merlin.

Williamson, O.E. (1978), *Markets and Hierarchies*, Prentice Hall.

Woodward, J. (1965), *Industrial Organization: Theory and Practice*, Oxford University Press.

Woodward, J. (1970) (ed.), *Industrial Organization, Behavior and Control*, Oxford University Press.

World Bank (1980), *World Development Report*, Washington, D.C.

Zwerdling, D. (1978), *Democracy at Work*, Association for Self-Management, Washington, D.C.

Index